THE

PUBLICATIONS

OF THE

Lincoln Record Society

FOUNDED IN THE YEAR

1910

VOLUME 73

FOR THE YEAR ENDING 31 AUGUST 1980

Set, printed and bound in Great Britain by
Fakenham Press Limited
Fakenham, Norfolk

The Lincoln Record Society

vol. 73

The Minute-Books
of
The Spalding Gentlemen's Society
1712–1755

Selected and introduced by

DOROTHY M. OWEN

with the help of

S. W. WOODWARD

1981

The Society is grateful to the late Sir Francis Hill and to the Twenty-Seven Foundation for generous grants towards the cost of this publication and to the Spalding Gentlemen's Society for permission to publish the text.

Contents

INTRODUCTION

Professor Stuart Piggott has drawn for us very vividly the intellectual climate of England in the late seventeeth century when the Antiquary had become an established figure.[1] His close relations and successors the topographer, and field archaeologist, incited by a spate of parochial inquiries, and aided by the newly appearing road-books, and by the activities of surveyors and mathematicians, were to become familiar features of the English intellectual scene in the first four decades of the eighteenth century. In their pragmatic observations and experiments, in their 'museums' or collections of objects, they were reflecting the attitude to all natural phenomena which the Royal Society, after its foundation in 1663 had spread widely among educated professional men, and, at second-hand, among the watch-makers, locksmiths, and other ingenious workmen who were to be found in many towns and large villages.

In the early days, as readers of Pepys' *Diary* will remember, the interests of the Royal Society ranged very widely, and it encouraged its members and correspondents to communicate to those present at meetings an extraordinary variety of facts and observations. The *Philosophical Transactions* for the years 1695–6, for example, include accounts of a six-year-old child, in face etc. as large as a full-grown woman, a relation of a voyage from Aleppo to Palmyra, a letter concerning the spaces in the cycloid which are perfectly quadrable, two large stones found in a urethra, strange earth found near Smyrna used for soap-making, a list of the plants growing within the fortifications of Tangier, microscopic observations of *animalcule* seen in water, a review of White Kennett's *Parochial Antiquities* which had appeared in 1695 and an account of a Roman pottery near Leeds in Yorkshire.[2]

When Sir Isaac Newton became president of the Royal Society in 1703 its interests tended to be confined to the more strictly scientific, and the antiquarian minded sought fresh opportunities for the exchange of ideas and information elsewhere. Their hopes were realised in a series of tavern meetings which about 1707–8 attracted lawyers, parsons and country gentlemen, in London for court or law terms or for the session of Parliament, to attend the exhibition and discussions of 'finds' and the communication of antiquarian observations.[3] One of those who attended meetings in the winter of 1717 was the young Spalding lawyer Maurice Johnson, who brought with him his friend and fellow antiquary William Stukeley. Johnson, who was at this time only twenty-nine, had already dabbled in antiquities, but he was also associated with James Jurin, who was to be elected in 1721 to the secretaryship of the Royal Society. Thus he had a double tie with the major intellectual activities of the capital and he seems to have been fired with the spirit of emulation to set up his own society in Spalding. He had already, as we shall see, founded a Gentlemen's Club in the town in 1710; here the members subscribed to and read the London periodicals, and discussed literary topics, but the society did not assume its distinctive character until 1724 at the earliest, and was not perhaps at the peak of its development before 1729.

It is interesting to speculate on the reasons why such a society should have appeared in Spalding at this period. The town was already the major market town in South Holland by the time of the Dissolution of the monasteries, and the seventeenth century witnessed its further rapid growth. In 1563 it was said to have had only one hundred and fifty-four families, but by the early eighteenth century there were at least 500 families there.[4] At the same period Boston had six hundred and fifty families. This growth may well be explained by the prosperity brought to the area by the fen drainage and enclosure of the early seventeenth century, and by the emergence of Spalding as a port after the main channel of the Welland was diverted past it, and away from Crowland, in 1640.[5] Defoe's description of the town is scarcely encouraging, but suggests some measure of wealth:

Spalding another seaport in the level but standing far within the land on the River Welland. Here is nothing very remarkable to be seen as to antiquity but the ruins of an old famous monastery. There is a bridge over

---

[1] S. Pigott, *Ruins in a Landscape, essays in Antiquarianism*, Edinburgh, 1976, pp. 1–24.
[2] C. R. Weld, *A History of the Royal Society*, 2 vols., London 1848, i. 470, quotes examples of the continuing interest of some fellows in antiquarian matters.
[3] Joan Evans, *A History of the Society of Antiquaries*, Oxford, 1956, pp. 34–60.
[4] R. E. G. Cole, *Speculum Dioeceseos Lincolniensis*, part 1, *supra* vol. 4, 1913, p. 112.
[5] H. C. Darby, *The Draining of the Fens*, Cambridge, 1940, pp. 81–2.

the Welland and vessels of about fifty or sixty ton may come up to the town and that is sufficient for the trade of Spalding which is chiefly in corn and coal. The town of Spalding is not large but pretty well inhabited but for the healthiness or pleasantness of it I have no more to say than this, that I was very glad when I got out of it and out of the rest of the fen for 'tis a horrid air for a stranger to breathe in.[6]

The re-endowment of the grammar school in 1674, the foundation of two other schools, a 'petit' school and a charity 'blue-coat' school, before 1710, and the provision for clergy widows made in 1680, are all indications of Spalding's growing prosperity. In 1695 the town's trade was large enough to encourage some of the inhabitants to petition Parliament for its designation as a free port. Like its neighbour, Wisbech, Spalding had also become a desirable habitation not only for the merchants who traded through its port, but for a number of minor gentry, clergy, and other professional men such as lawyers, physicians, surgeons and apothecaries who served the neighbouring rural areas, and for the surveyors and drainage engineers attracted by the opportunities for further work.[7] This concentration of leisured men and of those with professional expertise, provided Maurice Johnson with a suitable field for his own ambitious plans; the records of the society he founded reflect very faithfully the community in which it functioned.

Johnson represented in his own person many of the strands to be seen in the town society of his day. He was a barrister, active in the court of Sewers and in Quarter Sessions as a landowner, rather than a professional lawyer, although he regularly visited London for professional business during the law terms. It is clear that he owned considerable property in the town, could claim descent from the Oldfields, who were prominent Holland gentry in the sixteenth and seventeenth centuries, and was linked by marriage with many of the leading clerical families of the neighbourhood. He was a man of scholarly and cultivated tastes, who collected coins, books, medals, gems, maps, prints and engravings, appreciated Italian art and had a general taste for antiquities. Stukeley's obituary notice of him, which Nichols printed, represents very fairly what sort of man he was:[8]

> Maurice Johnson esq., of Spalding in Lincolnshire, Counsellor at Law, a fluent orator, and of eminence in his profession; one of the last of the founders of the Society of Antiquaries in 1717, except Browne Willis and W. Stukeley; founder of the literary society at Spalding Nov. 3 1712, which by his unwearied endeavours, interest and applications in every kind, infinite labours in writing, collecting, methodising has now (1755) subsisted forty years in great reputation, and excited a great spirit of learning and curiosity in South Holland. They have a public library, and all convenience for their weekly meeting. Mr. Johnson was a great lover of gardening and had a fine collection of plants and an excellent cabinet of medals. He collected large memoirs for the history of Carausius, all which, with his coins of that prince he sent to me, particularly a brass one which he supposed his son, resembling those of young Tetricus...
>
> Maurice Johnson esq., was in the latter part of his life attacked with a vertiginous disorder in his head, which frequently interrupted his studies and at last put a period to his life on the sixth day of February 1755...
>
> The family of Johnson was much distinguished in the last century. Maurice's great uncle William was register of the ecclesiastical court at Bedford, and created a notary public by archbishop Juxon 1661. Mr. Henry Johnson of the same family had a handsome seat at Great Berkhamstead, co. Hert.; was bailiff of that honour under the Prince of Wales as Duke of Cornwall, and game-keeper to several of the Prince's royalties. At Berkhamstead were half-length portraits of his grandfather, old Henry Johnson and his lady, and Sir Charles and Lady Bickerstaff, and their daughter, who was mother to Sir Henry Johnson, and to Benjamin Johnson esq., poet laureate to James I. Sir Henry is painted in a red velvet chair, with books about him, a fluted column at his right hand, festoons of vines and grapes at his left, and a gold curtain drawn behind him, a half-length by Frederick Zuccharo, esteemed capital.
>
> The family of Johnson were also allied to Sir Matthew Gamlin, to Sir John Oldfield, to the Wingfields of Tickencote, to the Lynns of Southwick, and to many other families of note and consideration in the neighbourhood.
>
> Mr. Johnson married early in life the daughter of Joshua Ambler, esq., of Spalding. She was the grand-daughter of Sir Anthony Oldfield, and lineally descended from Sir Thomas Gresham, the founder of Gresham College and of the Royal Exchange, London. By this lady he had twenty-six children, of whom sixteen sat down together at the table. Of his sons, the eldest, Maurice, was a lieutenant in the Duke of Cumberland's regiment of foot guards, and served under his royal highness in 1746/7 in Flanders; from whence he, being a good draughtsman, sent to his father and to the Society, whereof he was a member, several drawings of coins and statues. He was afterwards a colonel in the same regiment of foot-guards, and now resides at Spalding, and has two sons and three daughters.

[6] D. Defoe, *Tour Through England and Wales*, Penguin ed., p. 415.

[7] Some evidence for this can be seen in the collections of Sir Anthony Oldfield (CUL Dd. 9. 43), which include a long list of books in his own house, and in the Town library at Spalding.

[8] John Nichols, *Bibliotheca Topographica Britannica*, 1790.

*Walter the second son of the founder of this Society, was called to the degree of barrister-at-law and admitted F.A.S. (i.e F.S.A.) 1749, and treasurer of the Society at Spalding, where he practised in full business, and died 1779 leaving only one son, Fairfax, who is now living at Spalding, to whom we are obliged for this account of his family. The third, Martin, was in the navy, and died young. The fourth, John was educated at St. John's College, Cambridge, ordained deacon and curate of Ramsey in the county of Huntingdon, 1745, of which church he then sent an account to the Society, and afterwards vicar of Moulton, which is in the gift of the family, minister of Spalding, F.A.S. 1748, and president of this Society 1757, about which time he died. His fifth and youngest son, Henry Eustace was a factor in the service of the East India Company, and F.A.S. 1750; he died at the island of St. Helena.

He also had six daughters, who lived to maturity, five of whom were married. Jane, the eldest, married Dr. Green, who practised physic with great eminence at Spalding. The second married Mr. Butter, a merchant who retired to Spalding and died there. Catherine married Mr. Lodge, vicar of Moulton. Henrietta died single. Mary married Mr. McLellan, rector of Stratton in the county of Durham, and schoolmaster of Spalding, and Ann Alethea married Mr. Wallen of Jamaica, and left a daughter married to Mr. Stuart of Long Melford, in the county of Suffolk.

The founder's uncle, Martin Johnson esq., of Spalding, married a daughter of John Lynn esq. of Southwick in the county of Northampton, by whom he had a son and a daughter. His son Walter was educated at St. John's College, Cambridge, took the degree of Ll.B., and was promoted 1737 to the rectory of Redmarshall in the county of Durham, here he died. He was one of the original members of the Spalding Society, 1712 ...

Another of Mr. Johnson's relations was president of the Assiento at Panama.*

Johnson had a ready pen, and an even readier tongue: the earliest records of the Society show him perpetually contributing essays or discourses on his coins, manuscripts, or gems, and giving impromptu dissertations on the exhibits of other members. The so-called first minute-book, with its untidy repetitiveness, and its numerous interpolated notes and comments, which Johnson evidently added until its latest years, represents very fairly the uncertainties of the early members about their aims and purposes, and appears to be a compendium of loose papers, letters, and memoranda, rather than a systematic record of the meetings of the Society. It opens with a long dissertation on the history of Spalding, which Nichols printed, followed by an account of the Society's origins, which Johnson evidently added towards the end of his life:

From the time of the foundation of the Spalding Gentlemen's Society in 1709 'twas onely a meeting at a coffeehouse upon tryal how such an designe might succeed, to the time when it was fixed upon rules signed or subscribed in 1712. Yet I constantly kept every paper communicated to the company and read and left there, tho' these being for the most part printed papers, no minutes were made thereof. Upon the proposals being signed or subscribed I attempted taking minutes that some account might appear to be serviceable for conducting this good designe and assisting other gentlemen my acquaintance and friends in Lincoln City, Peterborough, Stamford, Boston, Oundle, Wisbeach and elsewhere to institute and provide the like designe and hold correspondence with us. In some of these places this succeeded, but wee had so little brought in by any member save myself, who constantly attended, and whether in London at Terme time, or on the Midland Circuit or attending the Isle of Ely assize, there or at Wisbeach, took care to communicate something literary every meeting, that I could make not much more out than I myself produced, as these papers (show) from that time when the following fuller minutes begin 2 January anno domini 1723/4 the space of fifteen yeares from my first attempt, yet by preserving all the memoires during that time (which are here compaginated) something I have found of service. The method of ent'ring the members' names present at each society I resumed in 1723 as follows and by entering some verses inscriptions and takeing sleight sketches by way of drawing some coines etc. endeavoured to embelish my minutes and make them more agreeable and significant. But in about four or five yeares left off inserting members' names at the meetings and left that to the treasurer from the 4 January anno domini 1727/8 as may be seen from this folio to folio 131. When I thought it needlesse to mention for the generality more than whether the President himself was in the chaire, or in his absence who therin presided for him as his vice-president, and the number of regular members who attended at every meeting and what honorary members were there, or other noblemen or gentlemen introduced, and by whom, or how, permitted to be presente. The greater difficulty under the circumstances of this attempt has been to render it useful and at the same time to support it with some share of dignity and spiritt on the foot of a universal literary meeting for the sake of improvement in friendship and knowledge, without views of any other profit or pleasure, the interruption whereof (as those necessities of business when all the presidents, *almost* were men of professions, and the young allured and drawn away and detained by parties of pleasure and amusement of dancing, cards, bowls, billiards, or the like,) rendered my perseverance and attendance more necessary.

* – * are additional notes supplied by Nichols to supplement Stukeley's account of Johnson.

There were several revisions of the original rules and detailed regulations were evidently agreed on only after two or three years. The first proposals were as follows:

STATUTES OF THE SPALDING SOCIETY

Proposals for establishing a Society of Gentlemen for the supporting mutual benevolence, and their improvement in the liberal sciences and polite learning.

That the persons who sign these proposals, and *none other* be esteemed of the Society.

That they choose a president monthly, to moderate in all disputes, and read all papers whatsoever aloud.

That they meet every Monday at *Mr. Younger's coffee-house* in Spalding, at two in the afternoon, from September to May, and in other months at *four*, unless detained by business of moment or indisposition, under pain of forfeiting twopence a time for a fund for books etc., except those who live three miles off from Spalding.

That he who is absent four Mondays together shall on the fifth communicate to the Society something new or curious, with an excuse for absenting himself, upon pain of being struck out of this establishment, if the majority of gentlemen then present vote it so; or pay sixpence, to be put to a fund to buy *books* etc.

November 3 1712 We do approve of these proposals and agree to observe them as members of this society

William Ambler	John Johnson	John Brittain	Edward Molesworth
Walter Johnson	Francis Bellinger	Stephen Lynn	Maurice Johnson junior
Joshua Ambler	Aaron Lynn	Maurice Johnson	John Waring

A fresh set of rules, not very different, was subscribed on 13 January, 1714, and this was followed by more detailed regulations for meetings:

The Aeconomical Rule

The Society must assemble at four

When the season requires there must be a table, two candles, a pair of snuffers and a good fire during the society.

There must be a pot of coffee of an ounce to eight dishes, or in proportion

There must be a pot of bohea tea of half an ounce to twelve dishes.

There must be twelve clean pipes, and an ounce of the best tobacco.

There must be a chamber-pot.

There must be a Latin Dictionary a Greek Lexicon.

All the printed papers order'd by the Society and not read publicly, and this book of Injunctions.

The coffee and tea must be ready at exactly five and taken away at six, which done, the papers must be read by some member, then a tankard of ale holding one quart and no more must be set upon the table.

The President must always sit on the right side of the chimney and take care of the fire.

Only scattered memoranda of proceedings seem to survive from these early years, and the meeting-place changed constantly. Formal records of meetings, such as fill the later minute-books, begin only in 1724, and run till the end of 1728; the remainder of the first volume consists of draft minutes, letters, and memoranda of the next twenty years, inserted at random. At this stage, as he said, Johnson introduced much of the matter, either from his own knowledge, or from the letters of numerous correspondents. The entries for 20 April 1724 provide a fair specimen:

Danceing wrote down or drawn in characters The secretary communicated the Royal Riggadoon, a dance, in characters. This has the music pricked over it and appeares like the characters of some Indian writeings. Mr. Weaver, in his essay towardes an history of danceing, says this curious invention was attributed by Monsieur Femillet to Thoinet Arbeau ... see also in Sir Richard Steele's works more.

Ms. Of St. Luke. The secretary communicated to the Society an antient Latin ms. translation of the Gospell of St. Luke the Evangelist on velom in folio with an interlineary gloss and marginal comment ... being the same verbatim as is called *Praefatio Hieronymi Presbyteri* in an edition of the Latin Vulgate published by Dr. Bireman. The treasurer said he had the same in Stephens' edition of the Vulgate Bible. The hand of the text is throughout the same and the gloss or comment of the same age and like it, but smaller. It is not divided into chapters or verses but the first word of St. Luke's short preface is written in green capitals and the initiall letter neatly drawn and illuminated as is the first letter of the gospell being an F around which a green serpent is twisted ... The book is complete and bound in oaken covers leathered over, impressed with Rhinoceroses and strange birds and naked men armed with bucklers and clubbs with winged serpents and foliage work and under a small square piece of horn affixed on the top of the right hand cover on the outside by four copper pinns is written on a piece of velom Evangelium Luc. The bands are strong leather sewd with green silke.

Weather; barometer and thermometer. Proposed by the secretary that a barometer and thermometer be provided at the charges of the Society to answer the proposal made by Dr. Jurin, a member of this Society, in his *invitatio ad observationes meteorologicas* communicated 20 February last and that the same be placed in the public library in the Vestiary and a table kept there to insert daily the proper observations by members of the Society.

While in London Johnson picked up, and communicated interesting details:

History architecture: and from the Secretary then at London the exact figure of the cone pyramid erected in France by G. Tourville esq., in memory of Mr. Seabright and other English Gentlemen killed there by a gang of Highwaymen.

Bookbinding St. Nicholas was the patron or tutelar saint of Spalding in conjunction with the Blessed Virgin Mary. Impressed on the leather covers of a Valerius Maximus bound about two hundred years agone on the one side the Salutation of the Blessed Virgin, on the other a prelate in pontificalibus with mitre and crozier blessing three children in a cauldron ... the book was printed by John Knoblochus at Argentin i.e. Strasbourg July MDXXI.[9]

Domesday The secretary communicated to the Society a letter to him from the Reverend Mr. Francis Peck with a transcript of part of Domesday ... relating to lands in Stamford Liberty with Mr. Moreton's and Mr. Peck's conjectures Thereon.

Engine for drawing The secretary communicated a machine invented by Mr. John Ingram, a watch-maker of the town for dreining the Fenns by throwing one thousand hoggesheads of water in a minute.

Old printed Ethides The secretary communicated allso a volume in a small thick folio of tracts ethical and prime impressions viz. Reynard the Fox, the Game of Chess Moralized, Cato Magnum et Parvum, Latin and English, edit. 1481 per Caxton, with strange wooden cuts[10] and a letter written to the Right Worshipfull Mayster Wapull by Thomas Hill parson of Tydd St. Mary dated May 1562 in a character exactly like the first printed book.

A few other members introduced other more varied topics: Mr. John Johnson, for example 'communicated an epilogue to the *Gamester* on Gaming, Satyrical, and spoken last night (12 Jan. 1725/6) at the acting of the play by Mr. Berryman, master of the company of strollers, he playing the Gamester'. Mr. Michael Mitchell 'brought with him and showed the Society the dissection of two eyes and the several coates and humoures thereof, with their proper uses and operations'. Mr. Mills communicated from a letter of Mr. Benjamin Ray's, a member of the society, an account of the laying of the foundation of the new buildings at King's College, Cambridge, and the poetry verses *in comitiis posterioribus* 19 March 1723/4.[11] Mr. Lynn communicated and explained three schemes of the eclipse of the sun which happens on Monday next (11 May 1724) 1. being Dr. Edmund Halley's. 2. of Mr. Whiston. 3. doctrine of eclipses in general of this in particular, supposed to have been composed by Mr. Browne a west country gentleman. Mr. Treasurer communicated a scheme of the same eclipse drawn by—Peper teacher of the mathematique in Stamford.' On this eclipse more was recorded:

The underwritten observations were communicated to the society and they agreed on them. Monday the eleventh day of May 1724, an eclipse of the sun was observed by several members of this society at Spalding in Lincolnshire the same beginning at fifty minutes after five o'clock in the afternoon from the north-west. N.B. the watches were sett but little time before by Mr. John Ingram watchmaker in Spalding by his regulator. At the height about an eighth part was eclipsed the wind south-east the afternoon was dark and cloudy. between three and four digitts.

The Reverend Mr. Bernard Goche rector of Croyland and an extra-regular member of the society 'complained to the secretary of a most notorious and scandalous abuse in the tenant to the grantee of the scite of the conventual buildings and cloysters in Croyland who hath dugg up above a dozen stone coffins or chests wherin some reverend men prelates of the church his predecessors or other noble men were interred scatters their bones on the surface of the earth and purposes to sell them for hogg troughs or other vile use.s. I went and was an eye witness. M.J.' Mr. Webber 'brought with him one Mr. Parsons an organ maker who gave an account of an organ he is now making at Boston, which, by turning as a jack orgainn, plays several tunes, but he has added to it the improvement of keys so that it may be likewise played on as any other organ and is fitted either for a church or a house'.

Local gossip is often introduced: The treasurer brought some of the white substance like plaister under which a sort of fine gravell was found on the surface of the earth in Mrs. Hudson's garden, over against the Whitehart Inn in the market place of Spalding. M.J. adds: this gravell seems to be the gritt of free stone and

---

[9] A copy of this work in 8vo was printed by Knobloch, presumably at Strassburg, in 1521, and is now at Trinity College, Cambridge.

[10] These three Caxtons, bound with three others, were still in the hands of the Johnson family until 1898, when they were separated and sold. All three were acquired by Christie Miller; their present whereabouts are unknown. S. De Ricci, *A Census of Caxtons*, Bibliographical Society vol. xv, 1909, 168.

[11] Antiquary and numismatist, 1704–60; secretary, and subsequently vice-president of the Society, *D.N.B.*

probably this was the place where the workman cutt the stones for building of the priory and churches. There were several carv'd stones found amongst it. It lies about two feet under the surface and then a bed of white plaister as pure as Paris plaister. Then you come to the gritt or gravell of which there seems to be plenty. Neare the place where this was found there formerly stood a church upon the abbey wall the remains of some arches whereof I did see layd open by the dismal conflagration of the town.

Mr. Stevens told the society that the duckers this day (20 June 1728) toke at one draught or push into a nett one hundred and fifty five dozen of mallards at their general ducking in Deeping Fenn.

Mr. John Harrison baker of the town goes in ice patins or skeets with a velocity and grace equal to a Dutch Hollander, a mile in three minutes.

Gifts of books flowed in from new members and are duly recorded, and added to the library of the Free School (the old parochial library) which was the nucleus of the society's collection: Henry Johnson esq. made a present to the library in 1725 of Heywood's *Hierarchy*[12] with prints, and Sir Richard Manningham M.D., then also admitted, gave Dr. Green's catalogue of the rareties belonging to the Royal Society, with prints, both folios.[13] The Treasurer brought in Gataker's edition of Marcus Antonius 1697[14] and Dr. Clarke's edition of Sir Izaac Newton's Optics 1719,[15] from the Reverend Dr. John Newcombe fellow of St. John's College in Cambridge. Mr. Collins presented the society with a manuscript Latin vulgate copy of the Old and New Testament according to the Roman communion, the initial letters of each book neatly illuminated at the end of the prologues.

Liber monasterii sancti Iohannis Evangelistes de Haughmond quem adquisivit Venerabilis vir Iohannes Ludlowe canonicus.[16]

By early in 1727 the society had settled into two rooms in Abbey Yard, and a physic garden was begun:

In October 1728 Mr. Stagg (the 'Operator') having according to order transcribed the *excerpta catalogi simplicium officinalium* as settl'd for the society by the learned and antient physician of this town John Hutton M.D.[17] a most judicious and experienced botanist, measured the ground, and the society having agreed to the said catalogue orderd the said Mr. Stagg to procure the said plants and set or sow them under the direction of Mr. Green who with the secretary now examined the said transcript.

The museum was also arranged in this period:

On 5 January 1726/7 the Reverend the president and Mr. Day having viewed Mr. Sparke's two rooms with the garden and offices made their report to the society that it is in their opinion a very proper place to remove into and that the roomes are commodious, being one for a museum wainscotted and pressed around, the other a withdrawing room fitt for our servants to attend in.

By September of the same year:

The presses being all filled up with lockes and shelves and the instruments disposed therein according to their proper classes by the care and direction of the secretary, the society was pleased to approve thereof and the secretary requested they might be kept in order and that the members would behink themselves of what they had to contribute towards filling them with usefull instrumentes or curiosities in art or nature and promised to bestow upon the museum some specimens of each kind out of his collections.

Another development was made possible by these moves, for concerts and plays begin to appear for the first time. The first mention of music is in September 1726:

Consort of musick whereof sixteen members and eight other gentlemen with many ladies whom the society toke the honour of entertaining with an agreable consort when they came.

Then in September 1727:

Mr. Thacker our tenant and servant to the society haveing desired leave to sett an harpsichord in the Museum, he being a musician and intending to learn to play thereon for our consort, it was granted him by the society, at the instance of the Reverend the treasurer, and now again the secretary repeated a motion he has many times made to the society that the musical gentlemen would bring or cause to be brought their instruments to the museum and begin a consort there every Thursday from after dinner about two o'clock to the time the society should please and that as those gentlemen have out of their private purses purchased Corelli, Valentini, Vivaldi etc.'s compositions they should be lodged in the museum and the treasurer pay for them.

[12] Thomas Heywood, *The Hierarchie of the Blessed Angells*, London 1635.
[13] I have been unable to trace this work.
[14] Thomas Gataker, *Marcus Antoninus de rebus suis*, London 1697.
[15] This appears to be the edition of the *Optics* included by J. T. Desaguiliers in *A System of Experimental Philosophy* ... London 1719.
[16] This manuscript is still in the Society's library.
[17] John Hutton physician, died 1712; M. D. Padua, F.R.S. *D.N.B.*

In succeeding years this seems to have become a regular feature of the society's activities. On 12 October 1730, for example,

> It was proposed by Mr. Willesby a member of this society and of the Music Meeting, as desired by these gentlemen that they may have leave to use the Museum on Fridays for the purpose the said gentlemen obliging the society with a consort there the first Thursday each January.

The minutes of a date in October 1739 give the details of one such entertainment:

> The gentlemen of the Music Meeting most of them members of this society with the assistance of Dr. Musgrave Heighington of Yarmouth, Mrs. Heighington and their son performed a consort of music both vocal and instrumental with which and wine tea and coffee the ladies and gentlemen who favoured the society with their company at Mr. Everard's were treated by this society as usual upon this occasion. The members of the society and other gentlemen sitting at a great table next the chimney in his hall, the performers at the other end of that room, the ladies in the staircase and parlours. The manner of which was thus: the society at five o'clock precisely was opened with the first music 1. concerto Lamparelli 2. cantata lisento per punir 3. Non se virtu. After this first music teas and coffee at about half past six. Then the second music, an overture in the opera of Titus Vespasian, an ode for the day composed and performed by Dr. Heighington 1. che mai d'iniquo Stella 2. Deh le piacer mi vuor 3. Alle fido.
> Wine round to all the ladies and gentlemen present at about eight, then the third music, Locatelli by Dr. Heighington, Mr. Lynn Junior Horace's Integer vite and Donce (sic) gratus etc. Dryden's Feast of Alexander set by Dr. Heighington, Wine round a second time to all the ladies and gentlemen at about nine, then the fourth music, Overture of Mr. Handel's opera of Malanta, Mr. Lamp's song of Zeno, Plato, Aristotle the music concluding with Alexander's Feast.[18]

In June 1739 a harpsichord was bought by subscription:

> subscriptions to the harpsichord inscribed Paulus Grimaldi fecit Messanae a.d. 1728.

The gentlemen's society by their treasurer	£5. 5.0.
Mr. John Johnson	£1. 1.0
Mr. Charles Townsend	£1. 1.0
Mr. Robert Butter	10.6
Mr. Thomas Greaves	10.6
Mr. Swaine	10.6
John Green	£1.1.0
	£9.19.6

On other occasions the town was regaled with a show such as Mr. Thomas Topham the strong man gave in February 1738:

> Thomas Topham the strong man of Islington: most of the members thought it proper to make a memorandum of what they saw Mr. Topham perform the day before 1st. by the strength of his fingers only rubbed in coal ashes to keep them from slipping he rolled up a large and strong pewter dish of hard metal weighing seven pounds.
> 2nd. he broke eight short and strong pieces of tobacco-pipe with the force of his middle finger having laid them on the first and third fingers.
> 3rd. having thrust in under his garter the bowl of a strong tobacco-pipe his legs being bent he broke it to pieces by the tendons of his hams without altering the bending of his leg.
> 4th he broke such another bowl between his first and second fingers by pressing the fingers sideways. . . .

Most of the information communicated and discussed by Johnson himself, and by some of the friends he introduced, continued to be of an antiquarian nature, and a few of the regular members made occasional contributions of the same sort. On 3 April 1729 a Mr. Collins exhibited two views of Crowland (the south-west prospect of the abbey and the triangular bridge) which he had painted for Mr. Sly of Thorney and a similar view of Thorney, drawn by Mr. Wood, was mentioned in the discussion. Stukeley's discourse on Ancaster, which he had prepared for a meeting of gentlemen which occasionally met there, was also read to the society and fully reported in the minutes. On 16 October in this year the treasurer showed the society 'a very ancient shoe or piece of leather cut like the sole of a shoe with cavities binding the same with a strap or thong over the foot, the leather is all of one piece and has been very strong. It was found in the estate of Richard Gerard esquire at a place called Ince Moss near Wigan in Lancashire three yards deep in the ground about four years agone and when first dugg up was very soft and much larger than now so that it would have fitted a good large foot. Not farr off were found wood ashes.' On 9 April 1730 the secretary acquainted the society that he 'had lately been

---

[18] Ambrose Heighington, 1690–1774, organist of Yarmouth and subsequently of Leicester, composer; *D.N.B.*, Grove's *Musical Dictionary*, 5th. ed., 1954, iv, 219.

informed that when some stones were not long since layd in the choir of Moulton church there was found but a foot deep the skeleton of some man or woman lapd in red leather covered with lead and a sort of crown or coronett on the head'.

In April 1739 Mr. Operator Cox communicated from Mr. Hepburn a member an account of 'a great quantity of Roman coins and a skeleton in a thick lead coffin lately dugg up at Chesterton Northamptonshire in making the turn-pike way, and in October of that year a piece of talc dug up at Thornhaw, with a tesselated pavement' and some coins were shown by the Reverend Mr. Ray. In July 1741 a Roman lamp lately found at Whittlesey and owned by Mr. Collins, collector of excise at Stamford, was mentioned and similar lamps ploughed up at the same place were described and drawn in July 1745. In the first three months of 1741 Thomas Sympson, who had made something of a name for himself as an antiquary at Lincoln, communicated a number of interesting details about the cathedral,[19] and in August 1745 Mr. Howson Hargrave sent Roman coins found near Nottingham as a present to the society. Meanwhile Johnson steadily reported on any local finds, such as the foundations of the old stone bridge at Spalding revealed in April 1745, and subsequently amplified the subject in June 1748 when he reported that his ancestress Lady Oldfield, in digging a cellar for an inn she intended to have built by the High Bridge, 'where the Blew Boar and other houses and shops now stand' had a 'gigantic human skull brought her with such teeth in it reported to have been Ivo de Taillebois earl of Anjou'.

When other subjects failed Johnson regularly fell back on his own discourses on the antiquities of the Courts of Sewers, or brought in a document or a seal from his own collections. In this way he has preserved for us copies of documents which are now lost, as for example an entry from the Crowland court rolls for 1330, shown on 8 February 1739:

> Also a very antient entry on velom from the court rolls of the manor of Crowland, setting forth the bylaws made at this court for fixing the rate s on ferrying from Clote to Crowland and thence to Walrans Hall 1d. and as much returning, and double of strangers in fair weather and treble in stormy and tempestuous, made A.D. 1330 ... and a prosecution by way of presentment in that lord's court against seventeen licensed ferrymen (*naute*) for disobeying those byelaws in taking more, in scandalum domini abbatis 1338. The *mala tolneta* or excessive tolls taken for passage or ferries were always an article of enquirie and hereby ordered to be given in charge to the leet jury for the process is against the offenders being 'naute de Crouland que naves habent ad deserviendum communitati allocati', that licenced by the lord in his court and therefore there responsible.

On another occasion he displayed and described what is plainly the record of the marks assigned to the bakers of Spalding in accordance with the Assize of Bread, in a very elaborately ornamented copy 'under candell the tubbe is a picture of one as at a table forming the paste into bread ... another weighing it in a large pair of hanging scales and a bran tub and dogg tyed with candles hanging over him.... And the baker schall be alowyd dimid.pd quarter for furnage iiid for jorneymen iiid.ob. for two pagys 1d.ob. for berme ob.for salt ob.for candell ob.for his ty dogg and all hys branne to avauntage'.

During a long period in 1746 the minutes of meetings of Stukeley's Brazennose society at Stamford for the year 1736 supplied much of the entertainment. They included antiquarian material like drawings of the gatehouses of Vaudey and Peterborough abbey, the skull of Oliver Cromwell's wife, a Roman camp at Wansford, Roman coins from Chesterton and a tesselated pavement from Weldon Northamptonshire. On the whole, however, the Stamford meetings seem to have been more concerned with astronomy and meteorology. At a single meeting, on 19 June 1736 the following contributions were all made:

> Mr. Laurence acquainted the society that by frequent and accurate observations by the sun and fixt polar stars with Mr. Sissons new invented transit instrument exactly fixt in the Meridian by Mr. Graham's royal pendulum he finds the latitude of Stamford to be 52ᵈ 39′ 0″ at Mr. Neal's the furthest house in St. Martin's the place of his onservatory. Having obtained the latitude to a great nicety as the data given, he observed on June 10th the sun's greatest obliquity was 23ᵈ 28′ 50″.
>
> Mr. Gilbert Clark a gentleman that liv'd in the house opposite to Mr. Neal's in St. Martin's, a good mathematician was the inventor of that curious and useful dyal call'd the spot dyal to show the hour of the day within side of a house by a hole perforated in the back of the dyal in one point of the axis. He liv'd about 50 years agoe.
>
> Mr. Lynn brought a large map of the visible hemisphere of the moon done by Hevelius together with another smaller one done by Mr. Senex. He gave us at the same time his observations of the passage of the shadow over the moon's face during the last eclipse of the moon when he remarked very exactly the times of the shade transiting the seas and mountains of the same, as seen from the telescope.
>
> Mr. Wyng brought a curious piece of the workmanship of a wasp found in a beehive being 3 globular *folliculi* or cases, one within another of a substance like paper, each having a large circular aperture in the center of this nest was fixt 7 cells in one comb, each hexagonal like those of the bees.

[19] Thomas Sympson, ecclesiastical official and antiquary at Lincoln, *L.N.Q.* ix, 1906–7, 65–90.

Mr. William Porter farrier brought a stone as big as a walnut, taken out of the bladder of a little Dutch dog. It was made up of lamine like the human calculus.

As we have seen, the Spalding society started as a literary meeting and Johnson frequently diverted the members by exhibiting and discoursing on books belonging to himself or on others given to the library. In this way he discussed not only incunabula (he owned Wynken de Worde's *Legenda Aurea* and several small Caxtons) but much modern literature. In 1729, for example, he reported Thomas Hearne's proposals for publishing Otterbourne,[20] of which he had learned from Beaupré Bell,[21] and in 1741 discussed additions being made by a Mr. Crines to Ames' catalogue of English printers 1471–1600.[22] In 1745 he read a Latin dedication to Archbishop Sancroft which was intended by George Hickes the non-juror for his Saxon grammar.[23] At frequent intervals, too, *vers d' occasion* and even tripos verses are said to have been read, though no copies appear in the minutes, and as late as 4 April 1749 he read to the company 'an ingenious copy of Latin verses on Belinda's recovering from a fit of sickness' by Mr. George Johnson of Durham School.

In the same spasmodic way pictures, engravings and medals were brought in, usually by Johnson himself, who at one time in 1729 tried to suggest 'the design of decorations' as a suitable subject for discussion in the society. It went no further but Johnson persevered. That same year he described and commented on 'a curious effigies of the Hon. Sir Isaac Newton knight ... made in profile in the manner of a medaglion by the ingenious Mr. Gossett and by him presented to the Museum of this society'. At other times, and especially after 1745, prints, engravings and etchings were exhibited and discussed: 'two copper cuts, one oval, made by Dürer, an etching by Teniers of a ballad singer "done with much humour," another of the Holy Family, by Callot, a block print of the Crucifixion cut curiously in wood with cross hatchings at Mentz MDLIX, a picture engraved by Mr. Vertue from a picture drawn in India by order of the Reverend Mr. Seigenhagen, head of our mission, at the expense of the Right Hon. Selina Countess of Huntingdon, of the Reverend Mr. Aaron.'

By far the largest number of the regular members of the society had more practical contemporary interests than this and the main subjects of discussion at the meetings seem to have been those which occurred to intelligent practical men in the course of their everyday business as farmers, surgeons, apothecaries, engineers, architects or watchmakers, or which they noticed in going about the country. Many of these men were particularly interested in the minutie of botany and natural history and the exhibition and discussion of the curious things they had picked up was a regular feature of the meetings. The third, fourth and fifth volumes in particular, when John Grundy reached the peak of his drainage activities, are full of such matters, and it is clear that between 1738 and 1750 much of the energies the society were absorbed in natural history.

On 6 May 1738 for instance, the secretary Dr. Green 'showed the society a beetle with the wings of a colour like burnish'd copper, of a forme almost as broad as long about ½ inch in length, also some lumps of lead oar very weighty melted with coales in a mine, brought in by the coadjutor and a strip'd large sharpe leaved tulip of 2 reds and a pale yellow having eight leaves 4 within and 4 without'. The secretary brought tulips, 'another of like colours but round leaves the same number ... these roots blew both in like manner the last year. For experiment Mr. Stagg now transplanted in blow into pots several of his finest feather and agate tulips to try what effect it would have on them next year.' A month later on 1 June, Mr. Grundy 'presented the society with a petrifyed egg or stone exactly oval and in the forme of a henn's egg which he took up in a dreyn in Arberton in Leicestershire and also another flat stone in an elliptic form, also a piece of firme wood dugg up 6 yards deep out of Jennsheath in Flintshire which is generally 20 yards deep wherein there is no record or tradition of there having been any wood growing'. Mr. Smyth on the same day 'gave the society an account of the method in which they intend to begin and proceed on dreyning our fenns, verbally'. Maurice Johnson passed from a deed of 1340, on 17 August 1739 to a white coot offered to him the previous Tuesday by James Weatherall, joyner, 'who rowed it down and so caught it alive in or near the Horse race common in this town. But he never having been able to tame or reclaim any of those sort of birds so as that they did not the first opportunity make their escape from him, advis'd him to present it to Everard Buckworth esq., who has canalls in his garden which is wall'd all round so that it cannot escape thence and is a great rarity.' On the same day: 'from the curator's Mr. Cox's hoppe ground was brought a sprigg of Hopps which had three large and long flowers full blown and out of the sides of each flower from between the leaves of the blossom several small green leaves, in shape and colour like those of the stalk or bind an instance of great fertility and shows how greatly this soil agrees with the nature of that vegetable which is indigenous and grows spontaneously in the hedges.'

In November of this year 1739 Captain Johnson brought from Langrick Ferry 'a piece of combustible subterraneous wood of a red colour like firr very thin and a foot long but cutt out of a piece much longer dugg up from out the earth and being very inflammable used for lighting pipes.'

Ornithology too was a continuing interest and there are many entries such as this for 2 February 1745, when

---

[20] Thomas Hearne, *Duo Rerum Anglicarum Scriptores Veteres*, Oxford, 1732.
[21] M.A. Trinity College, 1704–45; bequeathed collections to his college. *D.N.B.*
[22] This appears to relate to Joseph Ames' *Typographical Antiquities*, which was published in 1749.
[23] G. Hickes, *Grammatica Anglo-Saxonica ex Hickesiano Linguarum Excerpta*, ed. E. Thwaites, Oxford, 1711.

Dr. Green the secretary 'showed the company the greater butcher bird or mattagasse lanius seu collurio cinereus major, a small bird of prey of the hawk kind but of the size of a blackbird shott in this town'.*

Botany was a steady preoccupation of some at least of the members, and in June 1745 they transplanted to the physic garden a bee orchis in full blow found in a woody ground at Moulton when the secretary, operator, and some members, lovers of botany, 'went thither a simpling and to gather specimens for the society's *hortus siccus indiginarum* whereof they got above 60 several sorts and Dr. Green from them, and some specimens he brought with him, in Ray's synopsis shew'd the several kinds and their proper distinction according to that great botanist. . . . The apothecaries have a further use in thus going to see for simples in finding where they may either gather quantities of physical plants for their shops or to transplant into their physic garden here.'

The summer of 1748 produced much botanical and natural history discussion, cones of the larch tree from Mr. Middlemore's garden at Grantham 'which Mr. Miller describes thus: Larix folio deciduo conifera N.B. This is a native of the Alps and Pyrenean mountains but should do well in England especially on an elevated situation, a purple thorn apple, a locust found on the coast near Cross Keys Wash by a sailer . . . certainly a deserter or a spy from that terrible army of God which is living at present upon the most fertile fields of Germany.'

Medical topics, which from the time of a faked stone, in the first volume, had always been much discussed, now seemed increasingly to preoccupy the members. Occasionally the men introducing the topics were amateurs, like the Reverend Mr. Jepson, vicar of Holbeach, who on 4 May 1738:

> Gave the Society some account of Mr. Steven's menstruum for dissolving the stone or calculus in the bladder for the making the R. whereof publick Dr. Hartley who has written the physical history of ten patients cur'd thereby without undergoing the painfull and hazardous operation of being cut, has set on foot a subscription to raise the owner of the secret £5000 as a reward. The Reverend Dr. Stephen Hale author of the Vegetative Statics, a subscriber, has not from many experiments he has made found anything effectual for this end but what would be safe to administer inwardly. Seigniour Vagain of Cambridge, an eminent professor of chemistry in his time, after repeated experiments made for this purpose, declar'd the same.

More often, however, the medical topics were aired by professionals, whose comments were eminently practical:

> On 1 May 1740 Dr. Green a secretary of this society read to them out of the third volume of the late famous Professor Boerhave's lectures, MSS by the said secretary written when under him at Leyden 2° De Sensibus Internis the history of a celebrated Spanish poet who but a little before these lectures by a feavour and delirium lost all memory so absolutely that he was restored to health of body but like a young child forced to learn ABC again and afterwards being shewn some of his own verses knew not of them but was pleased with the composition.

The 'operator' himself frequently raised such topics, often in connection with exhibits sent to the Museum of the Society, and seems to have made considerable efforts to collect objects of medical interest:

> On 18 February 1742, for example Mr Cox 'communicated to the Society from Mr. Roberts surgeon apothecary at Canterbury and a member of this Society . . . a case of the cure of a very large and adhering fals conception, which he kindly offer'd to send and was desir'd to give his friend our thanks and assure him our grateful acceptance.'

With Maurice Johnson's death in 1755 almost all of this came to an end. The meetings went on, it seems, and entries, of a trivial nature, recorded gatherings of a more social type. The Museum and Library were undoubtedly kept together, and small additions to both continued to be made for the next century and a half. John Nichols the printer and bibliographer, had borrowed the first minute book, and made extensive extracts from it, at the end of the eighteenth century, for his publications, *Bibliotheca Topographica Britannica* (1790) and *Literary Anecdotes of the Eighteenth Century* (1812).

The foundation of the Lincolnshire Architectural and Archaeological Society in 1844 was symptomatic of a renewed interest in some of the topics which had pre-occupied the original Spalding society and it was not long before some at least of the members of Spalding were sharing this interest. In 1848 their president the Reverend William Moore read a description of the old society to the meeting of the Archaeological Institute at Lincoln, and subsequently printed it, with a list not only of the old members, but also of the 1851 society.[24] Besides the president, treasurer and secretary, there were now five honorary members and fifteen regular members, who still included three Johnsons, two Moores, and two Maples. With the last named family the

---

* In June of the same year an avocet was brought in, a young bird with a long slender bill bending upwards at the end, the feathers of divers colours black white and speckled with a long leggs and webbed feet of a blewish lead colour. Mr. Butter says it is a whilloc.

[24] W. Moore, *The Gentlemen's Society at Spalding its Origin and Progress*, London, 1851.

Society began to revive in earnest; much of its present position and particularly some of the finest items in its Museum, can be attributed to the long association with the Society of the late Ashley K. Maples.[25]

This volume was first suggested as a celebration for the Society's two hundred and fiftieth anniversary in 1960, and it was intended that Mr. S. W. Woodward and myself should produce a transcript of the first volume of minutes. It soon became clear, however, that the first volume was not representative of the series as a whole, and no attempt at selection would convey the quality of their contents unless a facsimile be attempted. It was therefore decided to reproduce the minutes for one year in their entirety, and, in the introduction to attempt to convey the type of material to be found in the rest.

In preparing this volume I have had very generous help from many friends and colleagues in Lincoln and in Cambridge, and especially from Joan Varley, Kathleen Major, Derek Williams, David McKitterick, and my husband. The officers of the Society have been my friends since, in 1954, I made my first exploration of the riches of their collections; I am particularly grateful to the late G. N. Bailey, to R. N. Whiston, N. Leverton, N. Simson, and S. W. Woodward all of whom have displayed more than kindness to me. I am proud to remember that they did me the honour to elect me an honorary member of the Society.

[25] The manuscript collections at Spalding were described in *LAOR* 6 (1954–5), 63–5, and *LAOR* 8 (1956–7), 65–8.

The Reverd. Mr Walter Johnson LLB, VP. in the Chair & VIII Other Regular Members & M Johnson Jun & Mr Joseph Hinson permitted to be psent.

The Society was opend with a Concert by ye Gent in cons of their Usd & Room and the Soc. had the pleasure of Entertaing the Ladies thereat with Tea & Coffee & co

The Treasurer brought in his Acctt & the Balln thereof as Audited by the Seer. & allowed Amounted to the Sume of £ 28 : 14 : 9¼ due to the Society.

Treasurrs Acctts

He also shewd the Soc. a very neat drawing with black ledd on paper made by Mr Seer. Green wch he recd in a Lr from him dat 3 Janry inst NS. of — SIGEBERTUS HAVERCAMPUS. HI: EL: LI: GR: PR:

Lr & Dr of Seer Green's

In that Lr the Said Seer. Says the ℞ of the Medal of Faustina posthuma is a Dogg running & an Arrow lying on the Ground. of which Medal being very rare, this Sketh is made from what he Sent in a former Lr mentioned in the Mind of ye Soc. 9 Mar ult, Constantij &as & Faustine.

Medal of Faustina Posthuma. Alarick Antiochus Soter filia posthuma & Lord.

Sigibert Havercamps / Dn ATHALARICVS REX / CONSTANTIA POSTVMA / ANTIOCHVS SOTER:

This Medal of Alarick is there said to have been struck upon the peace concluded between him & the Emperor Justinian, for wch the Epistle of Aurel Cassiodore is referrd to.

I have endeavourd to present ye Soc. in the 1st of these with some resemblance of Havercamp because he publishd yt Noble Edition of Josephus which were enriched with by the munificence of Joseph Banks Esq, a Member of ye Soc. & which conteines Dr Hudsons, His Oron & many other learned Mens Observations.

Havercamp Editor of Josephus &

Beaupré Bell Junr Esq, a learned Member of this Soc. has an Edition of Eutropius publlished by him, collated with an Excellent MS. at Trinity Coll. in Cambridge

Eutropius

The Revd Mr Gagnier near ye Theatre in Oxford understands the Malabarian & other Eastern Languages, we may apply to him for an Explanation of the Mission from the Coast of Coromandel & Tauto Letter on Cane Rinds, the former of wch was given to the Seer by John Ravenscroft Esq, & the later sent as a present to the Museum of this Society by Captn Topham a worthy Member.

Indian Languages

The Seer accordgto antient Custom read over all ye Rules & Orders to ye Soc.

Rules read

The Revd Mr Benjamin Ray MA. VP. in ye Chair & VII Other Regular Members & M Johnson Junr & Mr Richard Faulkner present.

11 January 1732/3

Alphabetical Scheme.

The Seer. comd the following shewing the Change of Characters & whence oc Letters were taken

Having Seen whence o.^r Figures are formed Let us now See o.^r Figures for Accompting

Numeral Letters I. II. III. IV. V. VI. VII. VIII. IX. X. XI. XII. D. C. L. M.

Arabick Cyphers

1 . 2 . 3 . 4 . 5 . 6 . 7 . 8 . 9

1 . 2 . 3 . 4 . 5 . 6 . 7 . 8 . 9

1 . 2 . 3 . 4 . 5 . 6 . 7 . 8 . 9 . 10 . 11 . 12 . 500 . 100 . 50 . 1000.

1 . 2 . 3 . 4 . 5 . 6 . 7 . 8 . 9 . 10 . 11 . 12 . 500 , 100 . 50 . 1000 .

Borrow'd from the Arabians, wch used them for marks of Quantity, and were eminent for their Skill in physick many Ages —

MSS Oriental Alphabets. The Secr. Shew'd the Soc. MSS Alphabets of these Eastern Languages Viz.^t Samaritan, Chaldaic, Punic, Arabic, Indian, Iberian, Hebrew, Syriac, Æthiopic, Armenian Dalmatic or Illirian. written about the Yeare 1620.

Des-Cartes Epitaph Read communicated by The Revd Mr Ray a Member the Epitaph of the celeb. ated French philosopher Renatus des Cartes upon his Monument in the Church of St Genevieve in Paris, written in elegant Letter

In Sequana Fluvium Inclitam Parisiorum Urbem præter= Labentem this Compliment on the Seine by Monsr Santeuil in Gold Let.^{rs} on Black Marble set in Nostre Dame Bridge in Paris

Sequana cum primum Reginæ allabitur Urbi,
Tardat præcipites ambitiosus ~~Opes~~ aquas.
Captus amore Loci, Cursum obliviscitur anceps
Quo fluat, & dulces nectit in Urbe moras.
Hinc varios implens, Fluctu subeunte, Canales
Fons fieri gaudet, Qui modo flumen erat.
Anno M.DC.LXXVI. Santeüil!

In Tybrim

Ego dum pleno quem flumine verris
Stringentem Ripas, & pinguia Culta Secantem
Cæruleus Thybris cælo gratissimus amnis
Hic mihi magna Domus celsis caput urbibus exit. Virgil.

a Stamford Almanacke Mr Butter a Member shew'd ye Soc. An Almanacke Titled POND 1625. calculated for the Antient & famous Burrough Towne of Stamford, wherein ag.^t the 15.th of OCTOBER is a MS Note in this hand

Fullney Chapell This day a grave stone was taken upp neere unto the oke tree in Chappell groone neere to ffulney howse — Hence Its evident that there was formerly a Chapell & Cemetery there wherein they used the Right of de Sepulture, as in several Others within this parish appeares by Tomb Stones, wch are still Standing or have been digg upp, at Cowbitt, Ayscough Feehall, Wykeham Hall

Chapell Green In the Accounts of the Town Burbay.^{rs} & Feoffees for the Poor of Spalding fol 5.6 of the guift of Gamlyn who was Owner of Fullney hall — A Peice of Ground called Chapell Green in Fullney the Common or Common Way East West & North the Undertakers called the Lords Dreyn South in Occupaten of William Wilson at 10.^s p.^{annum} — the Adventurers for Dreyning the Fenns used to hire this Aid in the D.^o Accounts 1731 ye acting Town husband's Charge rec.^d of Mr John Weyman for Chapell Green 10.^s ye Town rent

2

The Revᵈ Mr Walter Johnson LL.B. V.P. & Eight Other Regular Members 18 January
And Mr Austen, Mr Rd Falckner & Mr Johnson Jun. ſimille diſto be preſent. 1732/3

Jus Sepulturæ & de Capellis

Sepulchra erant Fornices, ſive Antra concamerata in quorum Parietibus circumcircà Loculi exiſtebant, in quibus Singulæ pluresve URNÆ cum defunctorum cineribus locatæ fuerunt, exterius clauſæ Tabellis Marmoreis, in quibus Nomina depoſitorum de more erant adſcripta. Hildebr. compend. 389. l.i.D. de Religios. Ut autem Celsus ait, non totus qui Sepulturæ deſtinatus eſt, Locus religiosus fit, ſed quatenus Corpus humanum eſt. pompon. in l. Locum D. de relig. & Junipt. Jun. pratæ 517. ait Sepulchrum eſt ubi Corpus (puta Sepulti) aut Oſſa (puta Cremati) hominis condita ſunt. Hæc videntur fuiſſe vel Univerſa, omnibus communia; Familiaria, quæ quis ſuis ſumptibus Familiæ ſuæ conſtituit; vel quæ Paterfamilias jure hæreditario acquiſivit d.l.5.D 6 de Eodem, hine in Inſcriptionibus Sepulchralibus ſequent legimus — SIBI ET SVIS. M.P. Monumentum vel Marmora, poſuit vel paravit; vel deniq; Singula, Sumptibus alicujus pro Seipſo aut quibusdam aliis paucis tantum paraᵗᵃ, hine legimus etiam — H.M.H.N.S. Hoc Monumentum Hæredes non Sequitur. H.O.S.E.H.N.S. Hæc Ollarum Schola ext. Hæred. non Sequitur. Flechi Syllog. 191. 257.

Monumentum licere deo Sequitur

Sepulchr quid. & ubi olim

Sepulchri Appellatione, Omnis Sepulturæ Locus continetur, præterea Statua Monumentum & Oſſuaria, l.i.ij.iij § Sepulchri. de Sepul. viol. Ulpian in l.Loc. del Reb. ſeden Spiegelium 537. Hæc Sepulchra olim prope Vias Regias, valente autem Christianitate in Cœmeteriis Basilicas & Ecclias circumentibus, deniq; ipsis proh pudor! Edificiis illis Sacris fiebant, & tractu Temporis in Capellis, etiam domeſticis. Vide Actus Episcopalis Fundationis Cœmeterii ½ Reverendiſſ Dñ Johem Whitgiſt Cant. Epüm, & Conſecrationis alius apud Lambeth ½ Teniſon. Et licencia ad Sepeliendum in Cœmiterio Capellæ de Ringmere, Salvis Juribus tam in Mortuariis quam in Oblationibus, & Obventionibus & aliis quibuscunque Matricis Eccleſiæ de Suth Malling in Com Kant. ½ Peccham ao XI. 1283. App. Gibr. Cod. to 24.

Magñ Sax: in Cœmeteriis Sepulti

Ea erat (ait Steph. Durantius de Ritib. Ecclæ c.23.) Vet Patrum religio cavere diligenter, ne intra Ecclesiam defunctorum Corpora Sepelirentur. Constantinus magno honore affectu ½ pro foribus piscatoris Corpus ejus Sepulturæ mandatum fuerit, factus, ſit Janitor; & olim temporibus priscis Saxonicis Rectores tantum in porticibus Eccleſiarum ſepeliebantur, Reliqui quamvis Magnᵗˢ (Ut Algarus Merciæ Regulus apð Oppidum Sui Nominis, Dñus Johes de Sto Yvone apð Petiburgum, Dñi Foreſtarii cujuſdam Magni cum Uxore Suâ apð Glynton in Com Northum) in Cœmeteriis. Miſſa non fieret aliquo ſine Licentiâ Epi, Miſſa autem fiebat Capellis etiam domeſticis ½ pro Mortuis, ergo Capellæ iſtæ conſecrabantur, & ſanciebantur Licentiâ Episcopali, quamvis in Præsulis alicujus eſſent Ædibus, altare habentis portatile,

Statua, cum Armoria vel Monumenti læsa Hæredi Actione Sepulchri Violati dant

Sepulchrum ſive Locus Sepulturæ & Jus Sepeliendi in Eodem ut vidimus cum Familiare fuerat hæredes Sequebatur, inde (uti puto) accrevit Hæredi Non Viduæ aut Executori aut Ordinario aut Rectori Eatra Actio iſta peculiaris in noſtra Lege pro Monumento Anteceſſoris Sui violato, quamvis Monumentum ad aliorum Sumptus edificatum, & Solum eſſet Rectoris Liberum Tenementum ut & paries Ecclæ cui Monumentum fuerat affixum & in hoc Lex noſtra congruit ait Cocus in Com ad Littletonum C.i.§.i. cum aliis Regionum Lt. & citat Caſſaneum fo.13. Conſ 29. /9 Ed.4. 24./ III.10. in Pyms 17 BC./

addit, Nota hoc genus Hereditamenti, & ſed nec dedit Originem & Rationem aut amplius quam Mirahur, cum Statuâ, Monumentum & Oſſuaria jure Gentium Sepulchrum continebat una cum Loco ſive Spatio Sepulturæ oia illa etiam cum eo Hæredes todem jure Sequebantur, & cui accreſceret in honorem Familiæ. perpetuandum Actio, niſi Hæredi ipſi qui ob hoc, inter alia, in Totum Liberum Anteceſſoris Tenementum ſucceſſit.

Communicated by Mr Butter a Member, (who was pleas'd to enrich the Secr Coll therewith) this Coine of the Emperour CAIUS. PUBLIUS. LICINIUS GALLIENUS Son of Valerian who was taken & made a footstool by Sapor Kg of Persia this Coin is curious being struck on his bestowing a Quantity of Corne on the Poor, & Ceres with Corne & a Flaile. V. Occo. 322. LIBERAL. AVG on the same Occasion. It is of Billion & has been Silver'd over. He was then a Prince of great Ingenuity & abilities, but became Effeminate & lost great part of the Empire, 30 Tyrants, some Women, usurping Provinces from him

Urbis
Lemovicen-
sium Arm̃

Sᵗhus Martialis

S ♋

Urbis Lemovicensium Armoria ex Sigillo f̃ 1 Fayanum MD. The Tutelar St of Lymoges in France is St Martial to wᵐ ye Great Ch. is dedicated, & who is here represented the S & ♋ Signifying Stus Martialis. v. Jauß Alt: 1632. Wᶜ Characters differ somewᵗ from the Francick in dean Hickes Alph. in Gram: Franco theotisca to. 3. and seem a mixture of Saxon & Gothick. And As the Heathen used Images of their favourite and Tutelar deities as devices both on their Coines & Seales, So do several Sovereignes & Cities of their Sts to wᵐ their Families are devoted, or Chief Churches consecrated.

Lr from
mr B Bell

The Secr read to ye Soc. part of a Lr to him from Mr B Bell a Member dated from Beaupré hall House. 15 Inst. wherein he says he is longer detained a Large Brass Cast which he takes to be the head of Antinous & desires to keep It till he can Experiment Its Specifick Gravity, intending to insert a paragraph in his preface to his Tabulæ Augustæ concerning ye Weights of Stamp'd & Cast Metal when tryed by ye Hydrostatic Ballance. & sent the Secr a cast of

CONSTANTIN
-VS. 6 &
ROMANVS

a rare Medal Inscribed CONSTANT. ET. ROMAN. AUTT. bA. The heads of Constantinus VI. Porphyrogenitus Son of Leo ye wise & Romanus IHS XPS. REX. REGNANTIVM. an head of Christ. The Original is Silver or Billon, in which Metal, this Coine is the only one known to be Extant.

Heraldry
Arms of
Bell, Beaupré,
Sᵗ Omer, Calthrops

Also several Coats of Armes curiously drawn & Blazon'd as Quarterd & Impaled with his own Family the Bell in painted Glass in Beaupré hall & on an Escutcheon or Hatchmt in Upwell Church. AD 1621. & of Calthrops.

ye Revᵈ Mr
Stanyforth
proposed

The Revᵈ Mr William Stanyforth of Christ Coll Cambo MA. was at his own Instance proposd by the Revᵈ Mr Ray to be admitted an honorary Member of this Soc. a learned Divine well known to most of ye Society.

Correspondᶜᵉ
promoted

The Secr sent James Mundy Esq Cꜩ of ye Bagn̄ Bk. & S.A.S an Extract of these Minutes he Enquiring how ye Soc. went on to Induce that Ingenious Gentleman ... to Correspond & Communicate to us somethg Curious. It being ye advice of or late great Member Sr Iz. Newton to Endeavr by all meanes to promote a Corresponᵈᶜᵉ wᵗ Ingenious f̃ Some.

Mr Stevens, Mr Jackson, Mr Butters, Mr Johnson Seer, Mr Fawkener, 81
Mr Austin and Mr Johnson Junr. But no body in the Chair because there
were not 5 Regular Members present. But ye Seer shew'd them this drawing
& on ye Title of Emperour claimed & given long since to ye Czars —

Theodorus Iuanowich Czar of Muscovy from a
picture of him taken in 1642 by G. Fletcher Fellow of
Kings Coll: Cambr: & employed in the Embassie there;
engraven by W. Marshall before his history of Russia
Son of John Vasilowich, Bazileif, his Stile & Titles
as then given him by ye Embassador & insisted on by him
were — Theodore Juano Wich by the Grace of God Great Lord & Emperour of all Russia
Great Duke of Volodemer, Mosko & Novogrod, King of Cazan Astracan,
Lord of Plesko & Great duke of Smolensko, of Tueria, Joughoria, Permia,
Vadska, Bulghoria & Other, Lord & Great Duke of Novograd of the
Low Country of Chernigo, Rezan, Polotskoy, Rostove, Yarustlaveley, Be-
alogera, Liefland, Oudoria, Obdoria & Condensa, Commander of all
Siberia and of ye North parts & Lord of many Other Countreys &c...
he says he Expressly Saluted this prince by the Title of Emperour of all Russia
& some Other of these Stiles but omitted the rest purposely because he knew ye
Muscovites gloried to have their Stile appear to be of a larger Volume than
the Queen of Englands (Elizabeth) But it was taken so ill that ye
Chancellor obliged him & the Ey his Interpreter was forced to repeal all.
in Archdean Johnsons Cosmogr. published 1616 hee stiles the Russ Emperour. p. 267. e Pauli Jovii de Legatione Musco. Ti. 1527. 9

Theodore Czar of Moscow 1642.

Stile of Emperour of all Russia before Peter ye Great above 100 Yeares

Marshall Fletcher hist of Muscovie Cap VI. p. 45, 46

Mr B Bell a Member presented ye Museum wth a fine Cast of a Grand Medallion in
Silver in ye Seer Coll. on One Side the building of Solomons Temple, wth ye legend
✝ EX ✝ TIMORE ✝ DEI ✝ OMNIA ✝ ÆQVO ✝ IVDICIO ✝ IVDICANTVR.
On the Other Side his Building the Temple & the Beautyfull Gate
✝ DILIGITE ✝ IVSTICIAM ✝ QVI ✝ IVDICATIS ✝ TERRAM.
Supposed to be made in Compliment to King James 1. of Great Britain.
wth ye Seer brought in ye 7 Casts of British coloured with Vitriol, made
by Mr Saml Massey of Wirk & by him presented to the Museum ye
Allocutio GALBÆ. from the Great Brass, Homer's, Augustus's, Nero's,
Domitian's & Attila's heads from Intaglio Gemms, & Ganimedes
feeding Jove in the forme of an Eagle Ovals. All from good Originals.

Medallion Cast by B Bell & presented

7 Curious Casts presd &c or Mr S Massey

The Revd Mr Stanyforth was put up again being proposed at last Soc. to be admitted a Member.
Mr Butter a Member comd part of a Lr to him from Mr Christopher Fairchild a Stewd to ye
Rt honble ye Ld Lonsdale dated from Lowther in Westmoreland Cumberland 22 Decr last wherein he
writes there are Several Roman Causeways crossing that Country through the Moors
which in bad weather would otherways be impassable, And not 5 Miles from
Lowther in 3 or 4 Several places are quantitys of Monstrous Stones, of such Size
yt it is now past Imagination how they were ever got there, and yt they grew there
is not at all probable because they generaly Stand at allmost equal distances
from One another & mostly in a Circle or after this Forme and
5 or 6 feet above ye Earth like Stonehenge: and Abery British Work.

Lr from Mr Chr Fairchild

Grand stone work near Lowther

Mr Butter also shew'd us a Silver Coine of Daventry Annes an Eagle display'd.
also a Groat of K 9 Edward IV. posui deum adiutorem meu Civitas London. well
pserved the Quintets on Each Side of King Bust Crowned full faced

Coines Daventrie

Ed. IV.

Mr Stagg our Coadjutor & Gardiner to the Soc. Obliged us with ye Ornament of
a fine Pott of Flowers for ye Season wch he is to continue as an Acceptable Decoration —
the Treasr to provide a fine Vase for our Museum throughout every Month.

Flowers in a vase

j February The Rever'd Mr Johnson VP in ye Chaire & Nine Other Members all Regul
1732/3   The Secr. Mr Johnson Read to the Soc the following Acct of ye great Badius and his Epitaphs

De Laurentiados seu Poematis Petri Rosseti de Martyrio S'ti Laurentij, Erâ seu tempore
Editionis. Virginei fuit hæc quintum post nestora partus   in finem Libri
1515   Et nibus adjunctis Laurentias edita Lustris.
N. bonaspes T. puteanus suo compatri clarissimo. do. Jo. Badio ascensio
de Laurentia de.

Jacus Jodoci Badij   Imprime subtili Sanctum precor arte Volumen
Ascensij Imprr.   Compater Ascensi major in ære Triphon.
   Immortale parant cui Orela Fidelia Nomen:
   Omnibus Error abeit quo moderante libris.
   Nunc quicunq cupit Charitas geperire fideles:
   Expetit ille tuam clare Jodoce Domum.
   Petrus ob hæc Rossetas adit tua Limina Vates:
   Lingua Maroneos cui dedit alma favos. ad Initium

Poematis in Do. cui præfigitur pictura præli ascensiani & Venundatur parrhisija Badio.
in Museo Mr Johnson D. huj Soc. Secr. pulcherrimi impressi. Tit. De Nobilitate.
Jodocum hunc anno dm 1528 super viventem Henr. Stephanus et filia Nepos hisce Ele-
-gantissimis Epitaphijs parentavit in Theodori Jansonij ab almeloveen d: Vitis Stephanorum
Dissertata Edit Amstelædami 1683. pag 29.

IΟΔΩΚΟΥ ΒΑΔΙΟΥ ΕΠΙΤΑΦΙΟΝ.
Κεῖν@ ὁ κ̀ι Μόσαις κ̀ι Ἀρνὶ πεῖσα πονήσας
   παρισίῳ ΒΑΔΙΟΣ κοὶθείαις ἐν δαπέδῳ
Βίβλὸς μὲν Μόσαισιν, Ἀρνὶ ἢ ἄρσενας ὑός,
   Ἔργανα εἰρήνης, Ἔργανα κ̀ι Πολέμος.
Καὶ τάχα ἦ ἔσκε Πατὴρ ἴσων παίδων τε Βιβλίων τε,
   Εἰ, ὅτε Βιβλοτρεῖν, ἤρξατο παιδοτρεῖν.

Epitaphia
Jod: Badij

Hic Liberorum plurimorum qui Parens,
Parens Librorum plurimorum qui fuit,
Situs JODOCUS BADIUS est ASCENSIUS.
Plures fuerunt Liberis tamen Libri,
Quod jam Senescens cœpit illos gignere,
Ætate florens cœpit hoc quod Vedere.

Ejusdem Aliud.
Hac tumulatus humo, Sibi qui, jam fessus ab Annis,
   Sponte Typographicum congeminavit onus:
Luci dum Libros, Librisq ferentis Lucem
   Scripta Sui fœtus tradidit Ingenij.
Qua digna esse sua Nobis est laude fatendum,
   Digna Suo et Seclo Nemo negare potest.

Reod
Mr Stanyforth
admitted   The Reverend Mr Stanyforth was Elected upon Ballott an Honourary
an Honourary   Member of this Society
Member

Earl Stanhope's   Read the Epitaph upon the Right Honble James Earle Stanhope, lately put upon his
Epitaph   Lordps Monument at Westmr Abbey agt Sr Is. Newtons one Front of ye Choire
Poetry   also a Copy of Verses of the Rt honble the Earle of Orrory's on his presenting
   the Reod Mr Deane Swift with a blank paper Book richly bounde
   both Communicated by the Revd Mr Ray a Member of ye Society.

   These are published in a News paper called the Weekly Miscellany of wch he had
   three Several, but Nothing was read out of them that was political
   and as being News Papers that was guarded agt with good caution avoid'd to ye Rule.

Extracted from a Lr. sent to the Secr. in June 1715 by William Stukeley MD a Member of ye Soc.
—about 3 weeks agoe Mr Falkner a Mercht of Boston (whence ye Lr was written) raving
up some old stone foundations behind the Free School house, where is a Wall is &c had often taken for a Roman Work, his Men found a Square Vault abt 2 feet over se-
-cured on all sides by great hewn Stones, & in it an Urn abt the Bulk and Shape
of a Quart Decantor without Eares, filled wth red Earth (as they expressd It) wch
the Workmen threw out in hopes of finding money, Mr Falkner carryd home the
Urne wth an Intent to give It me, but one of his Maid-Servts threw It into the River.
Mr Samuel Brown of Lynn (but a Native of Boston) told Me since, in digging
in his Fathers Garden here, They found an Urne full of Ashes coverd all over
with Lead. These things are Sufficient Proof that it is many Centurys since
or Country (Holland in Lincolnshire) was redeemd from the Ocean, and I
often conjecture that the Road between Boston & Kirton being for the most
part Streight and broad, & all underlayd with Gravell, this Stone place is Stone
is a Roman Work, & to Me there is an Uncontrollable Evidence preservd
in the Great Stone a Mile off us, calld to this day the **Mile Stone**, nor
can It be questioned but ye Romans were Sufficiently fond of so rich a parcell of ground.
In the Margin I have given the Forme of Mr Falkners Urne, from the Drs draughts,
as described to him by Mr Wm Stennit (a Mercht & draughtsman) as saw It
with these Observations agree those of the late Revd & learned Mr John Britain. Jan. 1722/3
MS. relating to South Holland, & treating of ye 3 several Imbankations of ye
Romans, & his Sentimt of the Plant of Dr Stukeley's Mapp of this Country.

8 February 1732/3 —

The Reverend Mr Johnson VP. in ye Chair & 7 other Members — regular.
Mr R. Falkner, and Mr M. Johnson Junr permitted to be present.

It was proposd by Mr John Jackson, a regular Member of this
Society, that the Secretaries may invite, *or any other Regular Member,* The Rt Honble ye Earl of Deloraine,
Knightly Danvers Esqr of ye Inner Temple, Samuel Gale Esqr Treasurer
of ye S. B. A. Philipps Glover of Wispington in Lincolnshire Esqr. S.R.S.
Sir Christopher Hales of Lincoln Bart. Sam: Knight DD, Prebendary
of Ely S.A.S. Bennet Langton of Langton in Lincd: Esqr, James
Theobald Esqr Secr. of ye Ant: Soc: & S.R.S. The Rt Honble ye Viscount
Wallingford, Alexander Willson of Queens Street Westminster Esqr.
Mr Philip Wilkinson a Mercht of Hull, & Captain Edgeworth of
Theobalds to become Honorary Members of this Society, & that upon his
notifying their Acceptance of such Invitation They be therefore Members thereof

14 February 1732/3.

Captain Dilliod VP. in ye Chair & 5 other regular Members, Mr R. Falkner
and Mr M. Johnson Junr permitted to be present. & Mr Miles

Agreed then by Ballot that Mr Secret Johnson, &c may
have leave to invite the Gentlemen proposd the last Society
to become Honourary Members of this Society.

Mr John Rodgerson was at his own Instance,
proposd by Mr John Jackson to be admitted a regular
Member of this Society a Gentleman well known to most of the Members

February. 22 The Reverend Mr Wm Johnson VP in the Chair, & Six other
1732   regular Members Mr Mills Senr, Mr R. Falkner, & Mr M:
           Johnson Junr permitted to be present.

           Mr John Rodgerson was put up again, being proposd
           at the last Society to be admitted a regular Member. —

1 March.   Captn Pilliod VP in the Chair & Sixteen Other Regular Members
           Mr Mr Johnson Junr Mr Falkner Mr Austen

Mr Grundy's   The Secr read Propositions for Draining of the Parishes, and Deeping Great
MS. Proposl   Fenn in the Wapentake of Elloe in the parts of South Holland in
for Dreyning Lincolnshire by John Grundy Land Surveyor & Teacher of the Mathe-
Elloe &   matichs an Ingenious a Worthy Member of this Soc. a MS in Folio. attended with
Deeping-   a Curious Sheet of Designes of Instruments & Models to illustrate
Fenn   the propositions and therein referrd to Drawn by the Author and
              the Society did conceive the Same to be an Ingenious and Laborious Worke & Mr Grundy
              had the thanks of the Society refusing Coppy of wh he had a Nott: Subscribd by Or: — 9th: Soc.
Mr   Mr John Rogerson was upon Ballott elected and admitted a Regular
Rogerson   Member of this Society
admitted.

              The Secr shewd the Soc. a Drawing made by Mr Bogdani a Member of
Small   this & the Antiquar Soc. of a Domestick Vessell of the old Romans
Roman   found near Canterbury & shewn there by the owner Mr Frederick a
Cup   Member of ye Soc. 22d of last Month. It is of as fine Red Earth as any
              China – Mr Lethellier has a Patera found there of the Same Earth
Silver   Mr Frederick likewise shewd there a Silver Ring of many angles
Ring   with these L'enlayd in Steel ✠ TARAGEI DE TEVE
MS of   Mr West shewd there a Very grand MS on Velom in French of Boccace
Boccace   fall of Princes; wth fine Illuminations of Every Story, and his & Petrarchs
Fall of   Pictures written 15 April 1409. amongst other Instruments
Princes   of Warr there are pictures of Mortars.

Magnetic   The Royal Soc was presented with a Knife and Forke wch had been
Power   so affected by Lightning at Wakefield, That tho used a Twelve-
              Month retaind a Magnetick Power & took up a Key.

Proposals of He also read Proposals for Printing by Subscription at 5s Each
              a Dissertation Entituled the True and Safer Method. of Treating
Lynn's   the Distemper of the Small Pox as usede in like Cases by the
Method of   Antients Received & Restored by W. Lynn MB. a Member of ye Soc.
treating of
Small Pox.

              Mr Butler a Member of ye Soc. shewd 3 Cornua Ammonis brought
Cornu   from Whitby whereof he presented one to the Museum
Ammonites

              Mr Grundy brought in his Plan of Spalding curiously framed with doors
              to Secure it from an Injurys, and as Ordrd to be done by the Society And the
              Treasurer payd him for the said Frame & Carryage.

8

The Revd Mr Brainsby & Mr Ray. the Treasur. Operator & Mr Mr Johnson Junr. & Mad

Mr West a Member of yr & the Royal Soc. & Secr of yr Antiq Soc. presented yr Soc — mr Wests

with Weevers Funeral Monuments in Folio with Wooden Cuts 1631. — prcut of

Weever

Samuel Gale Esq, Treasurer of the Antiq Soc. & a Member of yr presented the Soc — Mr S Gales

wt Enarratio Psalmorum LI. Miserere mei Deus & CXXX de profundis clamavi — Donation

q D. Mart. Lutherum. nunc recens in Lucem edita. adjecta est etiam Savonaro

la Meditatio in Psalm. LI. Argentorati apd Cratonem Mylium. An. MDXXXVIII. 8°.

on the Covers are the arms of France & England quarterly wth the Crown over

them and this Inscription in gilded Capital Letters, a present to king Ed. VI. // — Inscription on

AVREA. DANT. CRESI. VIR. MAXIME. MVNERA. AMICIS. — the Covers of

AVRO. QVID. MELIVS. SED. LIBER. ISTE. TENET. — a Book

HVNC. TWS. ADAMVS. TOTVS. TIBI. DEDITVS. OPTAT.

GRATO. ANIMO. CAPIAS. QVO. DEDIT. ILE. TIBI.

Captn Pilliod VP. in the Chaire and Six Other Regular Members and — 15 Mar

mr Austen & Mr Mr Johns on Junr permitted to be present.

The Secr brought in & Set up in the Museum of the Soc. Sr Richard Maninghams present

of a Specimen of Mons I. Chr LeBlonds new Invented Tapestry being — Le Blonds

a Busto of Sr Jacn IX. from Raphael Charton of the Miraculous — Tapistry.

Draught of Fishs, with an Inscr thereunder. which is fixed in a very — Pourtrait of our

curious Gilt frame at the Expence of the Soc. — Blessd Saviour

Theod the Soc. Proposals for printing by Subscription. Rob. Stephani — Stephani

Thesaurus Linguæ Latinæ in four Volumes in Folio with con — Thesaurus

siderable Additions & Improvements, with a Specimen, the

price to Subscribers to be 6 Guineas

also proposals for printing Memoires of Affaires of State by Christian — Coles

Cole Esq at 2 Guineas a Book in Sheets. from original Letters — Memoires

he also communicated part of a Lr to him from the Revd Mr Neve Secr — French

of the Gent Soc. as petens and a Member of this Soc. giving an acct — Gold

of 13 French Gold Medals found lately in digging at March in the — Medals

Isle of Ely and one English. viz Henri. DI GRA REX ANGLI FRA. Per Cruce tuã

Salva Nos Xpe Redr.

The Secr read to the Society DALKEITH. a Poem occationd by a View — Poetry

of that delightfull Palace & Parke the Seat of his Grace the Duke of Bucleuch

the Revd Mr Ray commd part of a Lr from the Revd Mr Pegg a Member of this Society — Wakefield

desireing some acct of Robert & Thomas Wakefield wc lived abt the time of the

Reformation and whose Lives that Gentleman is publishing.

The Secr. notifyd to the Society That he had acquainted the following Noblemen

& Gentlemen with Its kind Invitation to them to become Members thereof — Honourary

and that the Right Honble the E of Delorain. Knightley Danvers Samuel — Members

Gale Esqs Sr Chr Hales Bart the Revd Dr Knight & Capt Wilson accepted yt honr.

9

22 March 1733 Mr Rowland VP. in the Chair and Five Other Regular Members and Mr Rd Faulkner of Lincoln Coll. Oxf. Mr Austen & Mr Johnson Jun permitted to be present.

Inscriptions on ye Gold Coins found at March French Coines

from the Revd Mr Neves Lr. They are all as fair & as clean as tho lately coined
1 Franciscus D.G. Francoru. Rex . ⅟ XPS vincit. XPS regnat. XPS imp: X∴D∷
2 Franciscus Dei G. Francorum Rex ☩ M ⅟ XPS vincit XPS regnat XPS imperat ☩ M
3 & 4 do.
5 HENRICVS: III DG FRAN et POL. REX 1588. ⅟ Christus regnat vincit & imperat
6 Carolus VIIII. D.G.F. Rex 1569. ⅟ XPS regnat XPS imp ⅟ XPX vincit
7 Karolus Dei gra! Francorum Rex - ⅟ do / N. 8. do
9 Carolus VIIII D.G Franco Rex 1566. ⅟ Christus regnat, vincit, & imperat
10 do. 1562. 11 & 12 do.
13 Ludovicus Dei gratia Francor. Rex ⅟ Christus vincit Christus regnat Christus imperat.

Mr Neve in his Lr. adds they are preserved for Sr Tho Peyton of Elme Bart Ld of the Mannor of March and doddington wherein they were found, & ⅟ Skeleton of a Man with them

Heraldry
Arms of ye Antient Baronage MS

The Secr Shewd the Soc. a Large paper MS. belonging to Robert New of the Middle Temple Esqr, a Clk of the Court Bk. and SABS. containing an Account and Arms of all Nobility or Peerage of England from the Saxon times down to Q. Eliz. in whose Reigne It was written and painted Ending wth Henry Norris Lord Norris. the Arms are well drawn and Emblazoned properly.

Urne, found at Spalding or rather a water vessl that lay in a bank or elevated ground lowhich heretofore the Sea is supposed to have flowed up

Some Labourers working in the Lands of Mr. Henry Everard a Member of this Soc. late Ellistones, in takeing up the Root an old Ash Tree found buryd deep in the Ground under the said Root an Earthen Vessell or urne abt 12 Inches found the Middle of this forme, & of a Course Red Earth

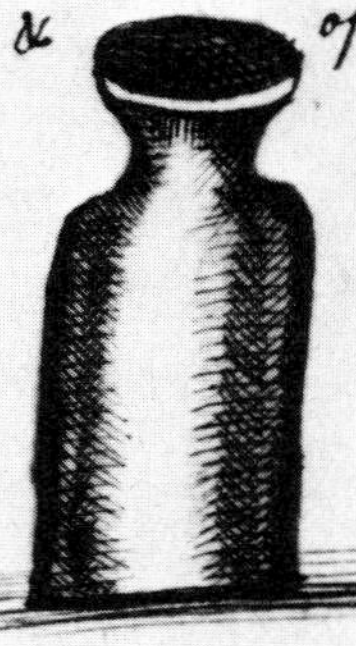

Mr Everard permitted it to be carried to his Kinsmans who there keep the Black Bull to be Shewn where the Servants brake, & on Enquiry for It I was told the Hostler had thrown it away into the Westload a river running by that House.

Carmen Hexastichon in obitum Sidneium

Illustrissimi ☩ Jacobi Scotorum Regis in Necem Dñu Philippi Sidnei Eq. Aur. Ulyssingiarum Gubernatoris Pralio Zutpheniano Octr 1586.

Vidit ut exanimem tristis Cytheraea Philippum
Flevit, & hunc Martem credidit esse suum :
Eripuit digitis Gemmas, colloq3 Monile,
Marti iterum nunquam seu placitura foret :
Mortuus humanâ Qui illusit Imagine Divam,
Quid faceret, jam si viveret Iste, rogo?

☩ forsan Buchanani, praeceptoris sui.

Mr Secr Mr Johnson has a portrait of him Hero by Zuccharo

Lusus Naturae in an Ash

Shewd them also a Lusus in 2 Branches of an Ash Tree spreading like Buckshorns

Petrifaction.

And a very large petrify'd Cornu Ammonis, Shells By Mr Buttery a Member v. marini Lister de Animal Anglia Lapidibus figuratis p.s. 51. M.1 Artic.1 Cl. Tit.1 pagina 205

Poetry

Read Mr Pope a Member of this Soc. his Imitation of 1 Satyr 2 lib Horace to Trebatius.

The Rev.ᵈ M.ʳ W. Johnson, Capt.ⁿ Pilliod, The Treasurer, M.ʳ W. Johnson Jun.ʳ
and M.ʳ Falkner

The Secr. brought in to y.ᵉ Soc. Martini Lister SRS Historiæ animalium
Angl. 3 Tract 1 de Araneis alter de Cochleis terrestr. & fluviatilib.ˢ 3 de
Cochleis Marinis Quib.ˢ adjectus est 4 de lapidibus ad imaginem
Cochlearum formatis. Cum Figuris nitidissimis. 2.ᵒ edit 1678.
being p.ʳ.ⁿᵗ.ᵈ to y.ᵉ Museum of y.ᵉ Soc. by B.ᵍ Bell J.ⁿⁱᵒʳ Esq, a Member
And communicated part of a L.ʳ from y.ᵉ learned Gent to the Secr. dat 18 Feb.ʳ
with a draught of a Medaglion. ΑΝΤΙΝΟΟC. ΗΡΩC. & Antinous lying on
a Gryphin with a Tuberous root in his right hand ΧΑΛΧΑΔΟΝΙΟΙC. ΙΠΠΩΝ.

M.ʳ Bell present

L.ʳ from M.ʳ Bell

The Plan of Spalding presented by M.ʳ Grundey was now fixed up in y.ᵉ Museum
a curious Impression a Seale of Venus & Cupid on M.ʳ Bells L.ʳ and of a Galeat head in M.ʳ Crausferds.

Capt.ⁿ Pilliod V.P. in the Chair & Eight... Other Members all Regular
M.ʳ W. Johnson Jun.ʳ M.ʳ Robert Austin & M.ʳ Falconer permitted to be p.ʳⁿᵗ

5 April

The Secr. shew'd the Soc. a Medal in the large Brass M. AVR. ANTONINVS
The Philosopher & a Sacrifice for the Health of the Emperor. a Priest sacrifi-
-ceing with a patera in his hand held over an Altar. & the Epidaurian
Serpent rising from the Altar.

Medall of M. Aurelius

he also shew'd them Imagines & Vitæ Impp Romanorum by Raphelengius An.ᵒ 1599.

& a Drawing made with a Penn by M.ʳ Johnson Secr. of the Arbor Legis
from a curious Print designed & Engraven by M.ʳ G. Vertue a Member
of this Society in honour of the late Judge Price, w.ᶜ drawing they approved of
as a good Essay after so great a Master.

Drawing after y.ᵉ Legis Series

12 April

Capt.ⁿ Pilliod V.P. in the Chair & Tenn Other Members Whereof One
Honourary And M.ʳ Wildon. M.ʳ Falkner & M.ʳ Johnson Jun.ʳ permitted to be p.ʳⁿᵗ

The Secr. read Some Mathematical Problems & Solutions commund by
M.ʳ Grundey. and Some Verses made by him on his projecting to dreyne y.ᵉ Fenns
also Shew'd the Soc. 3 English Coines. a Crown piece Silver ϴ EDWARD. VI. DG. AGL. FRAИCIZ HIBRAX
the King on hore Back (Under him) 1552. & the Armes of France and England Quarterd by a ✠
ϴ. POSVI DEVM. ADIVTORЄ. MЄV: the King has his Crown on, his horse Trappings adornd w.ᵗʰ
2 a Rose Noble of Gold МΛ RIΛ. X. DG. ΛИG. FRΛZ. NIB. RЄGINΛ. M. D. LIII the Queen
full faced Sitting Crowned & Enthroned with th. Scept.ʳ in her Right and Globe in her Left hand
under her feet MΛΙΙΙΙ within a large double open Rose For Leg.ᵈˢ the Arms of France and
England Quarterly in an Escutcheon Ж: DИO: FΛCTV: ЄST: ISTV: Z: ЄST. MIRΛ: IИ: OCVL: ИRIS:
3 another peice of the Same Queen in Silver, Sixpence or Teston, a Bust of her Majesty in
Profile in her haire flowing her Crown on, an Earring in her Eare and a "Ж" or Neck Jewell
on the Breast affixed to her Necklace the same legend round the head as her former and
the И as her brothers, with VERITAS. TEMPORIS. FILIA This is the first peice of Exquisite beauty coined in England
Since the Roman time and was designed by Valerio Vincentino a florentine Painter
Sent over by King Philipp to take her picture. There Seems in the Aire of the Face
a Sort of Gloomy Majesty even with Youth and fine Features. 'tis finely preserved

COINES

Edr.ⁿ VI

Mary

N.B. This day M.ʳ Grundey layd his Scheme (read here 1 March last) before y.ᵉ Adventurers

April 19 The Revd Mr Johnson VP in ye Chaire & Seven Other Regular Members
& Dr Wallis Mr Johnson Junr and Mr Faulkner permittd to be present

Mr Peggs Donation The Revd Mr Ray brought in I Ray Synopsis Methodica Stirpium Britannicar. Ed.3 cum Iconibus the Donation of the Revd Samuel Pegg MA a Member of ye Society 2 Votes &c

Of curing ye Gout by Oils. Also a Lr to Sr Hans Sloane Bart president of ye Coll of physicians & RS. about the Cure of ye Gout by Oils externaly applyd from Dr Stukeley a Member of this Society wch was read before ye RS. 1 Febr 1732 presented by him to this Society.

Melton Roos Gallows The Secr read a short Acct of ye Barony of Trusbutt & descent to ye Barons of Roos and from them to ye Mannors now ye Illustrious Family of the most Noble Prince His Grace ye Duke of Rutland. Giving his Conjectures from Records and Historians whns his Grace keeps in Repair a Gallows at Melton Roos in this County in Answer to an Enquiry concerning It Sent to him from Belvoir his Graces Seat by ye Revd Mr Edwd Sadl a Chaplain of his Grace then there in waiting by a Lr dat 6. Instant. V. Dugd Baronage 1 Vol. 542 545 551

V. infra the Lr at large entred 29 Aug. 1734.

Fenn men Subject to Quinzies & Pleurisies the Learned Dr Wallis of Stamford being present at this Soc. Sayd he had made it his Observation the Inhabitants of the Fenns were les lyable to Severe feavrs but more to Quinzies & Pleurisies than they in the neighbou-ring higher Countries — Owing to Great heats, drinking Water too splentifully —

26 The Revd Mr Ray VP in the Chaire & Eleven Other Regular Members And Mr Johnson Junior permitted to be present

Monumt 1300. The Secr transcribed from the verge of a flat large black Marble lyeing in the Middle Isle in Wyberton Church near Boston, whereon is pourtrayd a Man & his Wife by Strokes cut into the Stone, not in Relief. with these Armes or marks in 4 Escutchions over them Each twice engraven, there seem

Armes of Adam of Framton & Sibill his Wife not to have been any Brass for the bearings of the but these seem to have been designed Baron and Feme 28 Ed. 1. Ao. 1300.

✠ ANI, GIST, SIBILLA, LA, FAMMA, ADAM, DE FRANTON,
KI, TRESPASSA, AN L'AN, DE, GRACE, MAAL,
✠ ANI, GIST, ADAM, DE, FRANTON, KI, TRESPASSA, AN L'AN
DE, GRACE, MCCCXXV, LXXVIII YME, IOVR, DE, DECEMBR
PIIEZ, POVR, S. ALME, ✠

The Learned Dr Chishull told the Revd Mr Shaw ye Rector (as he Informed Me) That this was the Monument of a priest and his Wife, but I see no Signe of Tonsure, or a Chalice, or any thing in his habit to betoken him a Clerk.

Limning of an Auricula Mr Johnson Junr shewd ye Soc. a curious large Auricula Crimson striped wth Shewlet and a Limning of the Same in Water Colours on paper done by him very Exact this Fine flower is by the florists called Turners Duke of Cumberland

Concha Turbinata Presented by Mr Clapham Mr Jolley Clapham Chyrurgeon and a Member of this Soc. presented the Museum with a Turbinated or Wreathed Shell conteining a Quart of Liquid Measure the Spiral ending flatt brought from Asia by Captain Thomas. a Sort of Whilk, Mr Rogerson said he had Seen far large in West Indies but thicker shells

The Revd Mr Ray VP in the Chair and Six Other Regular Members and one
honorary Member and Mr Xr Fairchild & Mr Johnson Junr permitted to be present

The Carthaginian Language is not I think now known, even the powers of their
Punick Characters which Wee sometimes meet with on Gemms and Coines are
scarce known; the Roman Republick was so Jealous of the Fame of her last
Great Rival for the Empire of the World, That some think the Romans indus-
triously destroyd all the Books and whatever They could, that might shew how
great Carthage had been; the Carthaginians had themselves by a Law they
made [as Wee find by Justins Epitome of Trogus Pompeius] restrained their
Subjects to the Use of their own Character in writing as well as Language
& forbid them the use of the Greek, on this Occasion — Dux belli (that is agt
Dionysius King of Sicily) Hanno Carthaginiensis erat : cujus Inimicus Suniatus,
potentissimus ea tempestate Pœnorum, cum Odio ejus, Græcis literis, Dionysio
adventum exercitus, & Segnitiem ducis familiariter prænuntiasset, comprehensis
Epistolis, proditionis damnatur: facto Senatus consulto, Ne quis postea Carthaginiensis, aut Literis Græcis, aut Sermoni studeret, ne aut loqui cum Hoste, aut
scribere sine Interprete posset. Justin. Lib. XX. Cap 5., this renderd it more feisible :.
The antient Hetrurian or Tuscan Language used in the upper parts of Italy
is as little Known, the Characters seem better understood, appearing on
Vases, Images &c as the first Roman Letters inverted, but I never heard
of any Books or Writings found in that Language, or any things but
what had but few lines on them at most, and were dug up out of the Earth;
the Romans I suppose destroyd Every thing relating to Them early on
their first Conquests. To these wee owe ye loss of these Languages and
doubtless of many fine things wrote in Them, at least their historys &
Laws; the Remaines which could not be found and destroyd, but have
been preserved in the Earth, shew They had the Arts of designing in
perfection, especialy the Carthaginians; and no wonder that They
should, who traded to, and dealt with all the known Worlds ——

of ye loss
of ye Punic
& Hetrurian
Languages

Yesterday the Eclipse of the Sun was observed here by many Members of this and
Answerd very exactly to the Construction & Calculation presented long since to
ye Museum by the Ingenious Mr Joseph Smith; & Mr Xr Fairchild who observd the progress thereof with Mr Smith himself at Mr Dayrells new In-
taken Marsh in Gedney attested the same. that of the Moon as Mr Apator
affirmd answerd exactly to the Do Construction & Calculation according
to his Observation. Mr Stanyforth and ye Secr observd by the Solar Eclips
that the Dial near the high bridge accord 9 to ye movemt of ye watches
is Very true, which was set by Mr Grundy a Member of this Society

Dr Lynn VP and VII Other Regular Members and Mr Stennett
and Mr Johnson Junr permitted to be present.

On Leake Church bellis from Boston Mr Newkmit saw these Arms of a Lady
painted amongst others defaced - this supposed a Wife of Darby there
is ye remaines of a large old Mansion house there called Darby Hall
In Benington Ch. a large Font or Baptistery a Representation of the Trinity
And Images of the 12 Apostles are (as he says) carved
In a Window in the North Isle of Boston ch. in painted Glass. Sab. 2 Lyons
passant Or.

Mr Theo Brown of Horbling a Member his Donation to ye Soc. Lambins Edition of
printed at Paris by Macæus in Folio. 1588 a very valuable present

From Mr. Bogdani a Member the Secr. transcribed the following Inscription as com'd by Mr. West Secr. of SA & a Member of this to ye Soc. the Letters are Ex: sculped or in Relievo on an Ivory Handle suppos'd of a Whip found at St. Albans last year

Ivory whip handle

Ʊ pro Ʊ

ꓥ·Ē·DONATIO·GISLEBTI·DE·NOVO·CASTEL
LO·DE·IIII·EQVAB:·BENE·AꟽBVLAN
TIB:·QVAS·SIᖆLIS·ANNIS·DARE
DEBET·STO·ALBANO
VNDE·ꟽONACHI·PA
LEFRIDOS·ꓥABET

This Curious peice of Antiquity is now in the possession of Mr. Thomas Kettle of St. Albans, & is a proof of the great Value formerly (as at this day) sett upon the Northern Breed, I suppose these Mares were for the Stud as well as Saddle; Otherwise they alone could not be sufficient for the Service of the great Number of ye Monks in ye famous & flourishing house.: For the age of this I observe in Lelands Collect 2 Vol. 314 from ye Annals of Walt. Hemingford or Hemingburg. Canon of Gisebourn who died abt. ye year 1347. Anno Dni 1072 Reversus est Gul. Rex usq. Dunelmum, ubi Castellum de Novo construxit. that is Wm the Conqueror then repaird Durham Castle Infectoq. Negotio rediens Super flu: Tine Castellum novum fabricavit that shews he then built New Castle upon Tine. Cap. ix Ed. Gal. Sub ꓷ 1079 But there was a Religious house & Small Town there before in 1074. as is plain from the Same Author who Says It was thence then called Munthecastre since Newcastle. Then fol. 460. Camden Sayth the Castle was built by Robert Son of Wm the Conqr. Britannia Ed: Holland. fol. 810. (

Yorkshire or Northern Horses

Novum Castellum sup Tinam Edif.

Purple Brown Moth Fly.

Phalæna fuscié purpurescens

The Secr. shew'd the Soc. a Brown Moth of this Size on the Under Wings each taken feeding on the young shoots of an Yewe Tree. the Brown Seem mixed

a large Sport of Tawney Red (of a Purple in Some light)

a Fish called the Sea Snake

Mr. Operator brought a Slender Fish 14 Inches long of an Heptagonal form, with a very long Snout of one Inch, one Fin onely and that on the Back It was caught at Bosson amongst Shrimps, and when fresh taken variegated in Colours and Shined like Tortoiseshell, called by the

ye Back
Side: Sides
Belly

Fisherman who took It the Sea Snake.

a Section shewing the Heptagonal form of the said Fish much about the thickness of It near ye head

Which Fish the said Operator having gutted and dryd presented to the Museum. and as he observed must live by Suction for It had no Jaws, and the Snout as he shewd us by probing It was a long taper hollow bony Substance broader at the termination, as here drawn, It seemed to have no bones in the Body nor Scales, by this finely curiously distinguished with brownish Spots, at Equal distances.

and Mr Johnson Junr. permitted to be present.

Part of a Lr from Wm Bogdani Esqr a Member of this & of the Royal & Antiquarian Societies **Lr from** ***Mr Bogdani***
in Londn Dat to Mr Johnson a Secr of ye Soc. Dated from ye Tower of Londn to first

    I return ye many Thanks for communicating ye Labours of my much honoured **of Anglo Saxon**
Frds of the Spalding Society. The Inscription found in Sutterton Church is for **Characters**
Its Antiquity very curious, I should Scarce have thought any Monumtd in a
Country parish Ch had been so long preserved; the Letters as You observe have a
great affinity with those in the Inscription I sent You, but I confess my Self at
a loss to read the first word CꝜVI, which I think should be CY according to the
Sense, but the Letters are in my mind CNI which at present I do not understand:
Observing the Letter ꝏ makes me call to mind ye disputes that have been in order **Roman**
to determine the Origin of the Roman Numeral Letters who Used CIↃ to Signi= **Numeral**
fy 1000, I cannot Say this Letter is Roman but the Characters CIↃ seem **Letters**
plainly to be derived from this ꝏ & the D or IↃ which they Usd to Signify
500 Seems to be the One half of It, as well as 500 is ½ of 1000 & in like
Manner they Used the ½ of X which is V to Signify 5 &c. ½ of 10. I think
It certain that the Anglo Saxons used this Letter ꝏ & it is not improbable
that it was in Use here before their Times. as to ye part the Secr observed that
the said first Word of theo Sd Wyberton Inscr Supr a 26 April ult / CꝜVI was
probably cut at length by the lapidary or Sculptor as then pronounced for CY
being usualy written ICCI GIST, HIC IACET, Soin Lamaire Dict ICY ou je suis. hic.
CY ou je suis, Hic. adverbium Loci. Nebrissens Vocabulary English and Roman edit 1524. sub
Hic, says Adverbium Loci: en ce lieu. Sub Jaceo es, ui, ꝟesir estre couche ou Soy estendre. **Solar Eclips**

Mr Bogdani goes on. I thank You Sr for the Observations on the Eclipse of ye Sun 2d Instr. **at**
and could wish the Observators had Descended to Seconds in their Accot **London**
which would probably have brought them Nearer to ye Observn here, which
were made Very Accurately by Mr Geo. Graham & several Gent of theo
Royl Soc. as follows   Beginning . 5 . 14 , 45 ⎫ Apparent time
    2 May 1733   End . . 7 . 28 . 23 ⎬ Digits Eclipsed 9 8/10.
At London
Wch makes a Difference of 1 . 45 beginning & 1 . 23 Ending later
than Yours, which difference is greater than the Difference of Place **Dr Halleys**
of Observation can amount for. I would observe here that theo **Calculation**
Accot here sent You agrees to ye Dr Halleys Calculation to 15. **very exact**

Mr Johnson Junr presented to the Museum a Cast in Metal from an Impression of an **Casts of**
Egyptian Seal cut in an Hematites Sometime the Secr his Fathers whereon is theo ***Egyptian***
head of the God Camus the Egyptian Mecury (with a petasus on, & caduceus **Seal with**
before It) placed between a dog & a Cock . underneath are a Tripod & a **Hieroglyphics**
Scorpion   & under all 2 hands joyned, hand in hand   **Hieroglyphicks** **& of 7 others from curious**
also of Seven Others from Impression of other curious Seales in his Fathers Collo. **Seales**
Vizt of the Bp of Elphin found at Stampford &of Loudres found at Peterborough **Rom.**
of Inigo Jones the great English Architect cut by Gouoralls, & of Mars kneeling to Cupid.
of Apollo with his harp sitting . & Hercules killing ye Hydra & a Bachanalian Sacrifice **Greek**

Mr Vyner Admitted — Capt.n Pilliod notified to the Soc. That Robert Vyner Esq, one of the Knights of this Shire in Parliament hath accepted the Invitation made him by this Soc. 6 January 1725/6 of becoming a Member of this Society, and according to that Invitation he is to be esteemed Such, from that time And so declared at this Society.

Coine of Valerian — The Revd Mr Ray a Member shewed the Soc. a Denarius in base Metall IMP C P VALERIANVS AVG Caput Imp. Radiatum & Two Images in long Robes with an Altar between them PIETAS AVGG.

Proposed by Capt.n Pilliod That Mr Maurice Johnson Son of Mr Johnson One of the Secretaries of this Soc: be elected a Regular Member of this Society. He having made some drawings for & communicated others to the Soc. and presented the Museum with several Curious Casts or Copies of Antiques: and having been admitted as a Student into the hon.ble Society of the Inner Temple, being now present desired this kind proposal made in his fav.r might be entred

24 May 1733 24.o — Dr Lynn V.P. and NINE Other Regular Members and Mr Johnson sen.r and mr Richard Falkner permitted to be present

Mr Johnson Jun.r a Student of the hon Soc. of the In.r Temple was Put up ag.n being proposd last Soc.

L.r from Mr H Johnson Granada the Alhambra — The Secr.ty read a L.r to him from Henry Johnson Esq. a Member of y.e s.d Antiquarian Society dated from Granada in Spain the Second of last Month O.S. Giving an Acc.t of his Voyage to our Gibraltar, that he esteems that Fortress Impregnable & saild from Portsm.o to it spithead in 8 days, thence to Malaga in 17 hours, & of a Stone Aqueduct of 3 Leagues in length, and Mould run out into the Sea in 7 fathom Water there makeing by y.t City. and of the Antiquity & situation of the City of Granada & y.e magnific.t Alhambra Palace of the Moorish Kings there remain.g in perfection

Jupiter Assyrius Baal Peor — & brought in a present from Mr S.t Massey a Curious Cass from an Antique Intaglio of Jupiter Assyrius or Baal Peor Omnium Pater. in Profile to the wast.

Thomas à Kempis

In boecken met een Boecken

of his Book de Christo Imitando — Libello. a Motto he much delighted in & therefore placed over his picture. He was born A.o 1380 & died 25 July 1471 Aged 91. The most Eminent Men of his Age admired him for his Life and Doctrine, being of a true Xian Spirit, the Great Castalio &

Learned Men to w.m attributed — Stanhope amongst Others have given us most elegant Versions of his Imitation of which Wee had before an English Translation inscribed to Eliz. Vaux Mother to the Lord Harrodowne 1612. & there are not fewer than from the greatest Names to whom this Noble Work hath been attributed & pretty earnestly contested for by the learned Viz.t 1 St Bernard, 2 Ludolphus a Saxon Carthusian, 3 Ubertinus de Casalis, 4 Peter Rainaluzzi a Dominican & Apostolick Penitentiary, & afterwards Pope by the name of Nicholas V. 5 Pope Innocent. III. 6 John de Canabacco Rector of the University of Prague & Master of the Palace to Pope Urban V. 7 John Gerson Abb.t after.ds Elder Brother and lastly of Walter Hilton D.D. an English Carthusian & Eminent Author.

Thomas à Kempis a Canon Regular of the Order of St Augustin, & Subprior of the College of St Agnes Mount near Zwoll on the Oeder of the Family of Hamerken of Kempen in Colon, So well known throughout the Xian World for his Xian Pattern, or the Imitation of Jesus Christ; drawn by Mr Johnson Jun.r a Candidate for being a Member of this Soc. from the Picture mentioned by the Revd Dean Hickes in his Life pag: 34 in Rosweids Antwerp Edition 1634. pag: 35. taken from a Limning in a Velem MS of the Work & alluding to the traditionary Legend, as the Dean thinks unconcerned In Omnium Requiem quaesivi & nusquam inveni nisi in Angello cum 8 D.r Charlier & Gerson Chancellor of Paris, 9 Th.o à Kempis Prior of Windesheim the Author.

Capt. Pilliod communicated to the Soc. part of a Lr he lately recieved from
Mr Green one of the Secretaries of this Society now Leyden that he there
sees a Child of Nine months of Age that measures a Yard in the Wast
& is in other respects proportionable born at Haerlem.

And that they have in the Physick Garden at Leyden the True
Rhubarb growing which has not been long raised in Europe
with the description of It as it appeared when first It blew at a
Gentlemans Garden in Groenengen, & from the Botanical Authors.
This Letter is dated 16 Instant N.S.

The Reverend Mr Ray V.P. in the Chair and Nine Other Regular Members
& One honourary and Mr Richd Falconer Permitted to be present.

Mr Richard Falconer shewd the Soc. a Drawing by him made of the Pedestal
of Alford Cross in this County: And of the Monument of a Man in
Male lyeing within an Arch in the Church of Saleby near Alford, with
a Coat of Armes engraven on his Shield, which seems to be a Cross engrailed
and is perhapps designed for One of the Family of Mussenden of Heling in
this County, who did beare. Or. a Cross engrailed Gu. on the first point a
Cornish Chough proper. MS Marwood ten Boswells fo. 113. Yorkes Union fo. 111
The Parish Clerks Traditional Tale is that this Knight was Nibbled to
Death by Something in the likeness of a Pauder, therefore the Bird is
placed on his Shielde.
Mr Falconer also shewd them a larger Brass Seal of 4 Great Quarters
Counterquartered viz. 1, qrly. Barry, 6, Arg. & Az. 3 Torteaulx en Chief.
2dly Az. Cinque Foyle Ermine ● Astley of Astley or Aysley. 3d as 2d. 4th as 1st.
In the Second Grand Quarter. Or. Maunche Gules. Hastinges of Burgaveny
2dly Barry 10 Arg. & Azure 10 Martletts in Urle Gu. Valence or de Valencia.
3d as 2d. 4 as 1st. The 3d Grand Quarter counterquartered and as the 2d. then
4th as the 1st. × MS Robt Glew Med Templi Soc.
Reginald Lord Grey of Ruthyn by Ioane Daughter & sole heire of Wm Lord Astley
had Edward Grey Ld Ferrers of Groby John Grey of Barwell, Leic. & Robt Grey of
Enfield, Staff. which Reginald was Son & heire of Roger Lord Grey of Ruthen Castle
in Wales Maried by Elizabeth Daughter & heire of John Lord Hastinges by Isabel
his Wife the Eldest daughter & Coheir of Wm Valence Earle of Pembroke
These are the 4 first Quarterings of the Armes of the Right Honble
the Earle of Stamford.

An Impression of which Seale he presented to the Museum
& the Secr. also one of the Seale of his Kinsman Henry Johnson Esqr
Son of the late Coll. William Johnson (Broth of Sr Henry, Father of the Rt Hon
Anne Countess of Strafford,) & Son of Sr Henry Johnson the Elder curiously Cuts on a Topaz &
emblasoned by hatchings & in their proper Colors, bearing Eight Coats Quarterly
1st Johnson 1 Or. Waterbouge Sab. on a Chief Gu. 3 Bezants Johnson of Norfolk
the other Branch of the Same Family in Lincolnsh are distinguished by Martletts
2 Teyson Thane of Alnwick Vert 3 Lyons rampt arg. 3 Rouse of Grymleby Gules 3 Waterboug:
arg. 4 Attiric of the Same Gules 3 Fleur de Lys arg between 2 Bends Vary 5 Or. a double
headed Lyon Az. Lord of Nelson Arg 3 Cinquefoyles az. on a Fess gu. 2 pigeons or. 7. Argoll Baron of Craydon
arg. 3 Estoyles & Bord. engrailed Sable. Crest 2 Eagles Wings, one a dur Cornett. Motto PER VARIOS CASUS.

Stony Incrustation from Whaplode — The Secr: presented the Soc.ᵗʸ wᵗʰ a Peice of Petrified Root of a Tree or rather a Stoney Incrustation composed of a very brown reddish small Sand dugg out of a Sand Pit in Whaplode in this Neighbourhood by the Revd Chr Dr Tatham the Vicar's Servant, It Tubulous or hollow and out of It Mr Tatham told the sd Secr. he picked a Substance which he tooke to be pars of a root.

Casts Pyrhus Jesus X V. M. Gregory XIII. — Also with some Curious Casts Bacchus & Cupid in a large Oval & Pyrhus King of Epirus from an Antiques. Our Blessed Saviour & the Virgin Mary from y.e fine Silver Bulla mentioned & drawn in the Minutes 23 March & 18 May 1732 & GREGORIVS XIII. PONT. MAX. AN. I. IVGONOTORVM. STRAGES. 1571. on the Massacre at Paris of the Admiral Colligni & the protestants by Assassination. the Additions to the X Book of the Dutch Commentaries printed the Year after pag. 33 say. The Pope hearing of these Murders went himself with his whol Colledge of Cardinals first of all to the Church of St Mark & gave very large Thankes to God. Then the next day after he Celebrated a Solemn Masse & Commanded a Iubilee.

Julian de Medices — MAG IVLIANVS MEDICES. The profile head of Iulian de Medices. ℞ a Female Figure sitting on a Trophé with a Genius in the right hand extended between C. P. consulto Patrum. ex urg. ROMA. perhaps Struck by order of the Conclave in honour of Iulian Father of Iulio di Medicis declared Pope by the Name of Clement VII. tó Instigated Car. 5 to besiege Florence to Revenge his Fathers death Who had been assassinated by the Artifices of Francisco Salviani ABp of Pisa at the Elevation of the Host 1472. and fixed the Dukedome in his Family by the Emperors power, who gave It to Alexander de Medicis the Popes Nephew with his the sd Emperors Natural Daughter. A.D. 1531.

Christina Queen of Sweeden — CHRISTINA REGINA. the Queen's head in Profile crowned with Laurell. ℞ a Right Arm bare & extended as from Clouds holds the Sweedish Crown under It AVITAM. ET. AVCTAM. Daughter & heire of the Great King Gustavus Adolphus whom She Succedede at Six Years of age & governd bravely & wisely above 20 Yeares and then resigned to her Nephew Charles Gustavus 1654. and reserving a competent Revenue to her Self retired to Rome, and on her there being Reconciled to that Church this Medal was made. This Lady was well intituled to the Laurells for her bravery, her Victories over the Germans, Poles, Saxons, & Danes, & her great proficiency in all Arts & Sciences.

Mr Operator Cox communicated the following Inscription on a Monument in the Cathedral Church of Canterbury, near the Font.

Inscription on Tho. Blomer. an Infant — Hic jacet, Almâ pace Sopitus, Thomas Radulphi Blomer S.T.P. & Hestiræ Ux. ejus fil. natu 2 post q̃ aū Suavissimo tenore exactos, morbo antiquo et inclementi correptus & heu nequicquam invocatâ Medicinâ, animam D.O.M. placidissimè cessit, Divince particulam Aurce: fuit ille omnibus quæ tam teneræ Ætati competunt Laudibus cumulatus: Fide supra ætatem vivida & animosa, qualem denig leete ferebat, tali toto habitu vitæ moriens, emicuit, ut abreptum vel Lachrymis profecto viro non sit indignum, Ingens apud parentes mastissimos sui desiderium reliquit: Sed hunc tamen Pietatis sive dolorem sive Invsaniam multoties nsq Iucundissima Vitæ beatioris Expectatis: hac Spe fruantur parens

Patres Matresq; hae suos etiam defunctos amplectantur,
Vos quotquot hic passim discurritis (Ne hic quidem satis
Memores fugioutis aevi) Saltem hoc discite, monente Christo:
tanquam Infantes Regnum Dei excipite, Mente non elatâ
puro Corde, Simplici affectu, Salvete! Æternitali prospi-
-cite. 06: Iulij 8ᵒ 1719. Ætatis 16.

M. Johnson
Iun admitted

Maurice Johnson Iun a Student of the Inner Temple was upon Ballott elected
and Admitted a Regular Member of the Society.

The Reverᵈ the Præsident in yᵉ Chair & Eight Other Regular Members
& mʳ Richᵈ Falkner of Lincoln College in Oxford Admitted to be present

7 Iunij
1733.

The Secrʸ has wrote Mʳ Richᵈ Norcliffe a Merchᵗ at Frederickshall in Norway
a Good Correspondᵗ wᵗ yᵉ Soc. by meanes of Mʳ Butters a Membʳ And returned
him as Orderᵈ yᵉ Thanks of this Soc. for his Ingenious ansʳ to their Queries
lettd Aprill 1732 and ansᵈ in Augᵗ; with some farther Enquiries now sent
Vist) for Specimens of Cones of Pines & Firres, and Seeds of Trees, plantes
And of Shells found on that Coast, Sketch of Monumᵗ erected there on
the late King Sweeden's being killed at the Siege of the Castle &c

Queries to
Norway.

Doctissimi Georgij Fabricij Chemnicensis Epigramma in **Poetas Elegiacos**
1594.

Est gravis & cultus, puroq; Simillimus Amni,
        Dulciaq; Eloquio verba **Tibullus** habet.
Mollis & abstrusus, teneriq; **Propertius** oris,
        Interdum Baccho sed trahit ille pedem.
At facilis **Naso**, sulcans pleno Æquora Velo,
        Pectore Castalias divite fundit opes.
Hos celebrat blandos Elegiia prima Poetas:
        Diversi quamvis, laus sua quemq; manet.

Fabricius's
Charatters
of Tibullus
Propertius
&
Ovid.

Some Select parts of these Poets, called the Electa Minora, & Majora,
printed for the Use of Eton School, are taught there; They being by
Youth caute legenda, & therefore So Selected by the Masters.

In a Ms. of Affordby & other parts of this County written abᵗ the Yeare 1480

an old
English
Laud.

ffader of heven yat never begynning had.
Maker of the erthe of ou[r]y glootuy
of Resonable & unresonable both gode & bad.
And all for owr wele & eke to plessuy
of all maukind as scriptur doth remenuy
Whosoere blessed lorde we laude & hertely panke the
of yᵉ grete godenesse showed, to oper & to me

It is probable written by one mʳ Wᵐ Wermingham yᵉ Clerk of the Household to the Rᵗ honᵇˡᵉ
Henry Earle of Northumberland as appeares by this remarkable entry in the same hand
at the End of the Book. Exit & qᵗ di. brasiʸ in hospic Henᵈ percy Comit Northumbᵣ
Dᵒ RR E:4.ᵗ R:3. & H:7. 4 Pipe 1 hoggᵈ ꝪꝪ 42¼ lag. & aliq 5 pipe ʒtin' 4 60 lag. cervic
ꝑ quib' pip xx viij lag — Exit 4 qᵗ ʒ frīt, ix paus & aliq mayᵖ pond' cujusᵗ panis

the House
hold & hospi
tality of yᵉ
Eᵒ of North.

in ᵍhospicio Wᵐ Wermyncham fuit Clericus hospᵖ Spac 5 aᵈ di. tempor. Johis Everingham militis Wᵗ
Benett Clic & Wᵗ Ralston Conparotulatorᵉ & Seneschall & fuer cotidiᵉ in Eod de Genᵗo Valetᵗ y Garcionibʸ CCiiij ᵗᵒ

Small Brass of Claudius Mr Collins the Collect of the Excise has a Peice of Small Brass Coin pretty thick & TI CLAVDIVS CAESAR AVG ʒ̃ / 4 around SC. PON M TR P IMP PP COS II Mr Tho Burton Town Clk of ⌷SPQR⌷ Boston &c donated & adm̃d Regular Member this curious peice both for size and inscription under the Bilanc: was found at Colchester

14 June 1733. The Reṽd Mr Lyon President in the Chair, and Seven other regular Members, and one Honorary

Lr from y Secr. Communicated then to the Society the following Letter from Mr Mr Johnson Secretary of wt he he communicated to the Soc. of Antiquaries

Colville Mr Gale brought a Bull from Pope Boniface granting a Dispensation to Sir John Colville Knt to marry Emma Godeneye his Concubine sometime Wife of Willm Talmage his Kinsman & edward

Newton Chantry near Wisbeach Familiari d̃ñi d̃ñi John Colvilles And a Copy of the Statutes of a Chantry for 4 Chaplains 4 Inferior Clarks or Capellani & 10 poor Men & 1 poor Woman in Newton near Wisbeach in the Isle of Ely & County of Cambridge to pray for the Souls of H IV & Joan his Consort John Fordham Bp. of Ely, & pr & Convent of Ely, the sd Sr John Colville & Emma his Wife — John Duke of Lancaster & Blanch his Wife & Mary late Countess of Derby.

Heraldry His Armes as Illumined twice at the beginning which Sr John Colville Says he caused to be painted there —

The Arms of Sr John Colville

Sr John Colvilles papal Dispensation

The Notarial Mark on the back of yt An Account of the Copy of King John's Magna Charta. now engraved on a very large Copper Plate & published to perpetuate It.

Magna Charta Johis Regis Angl. Mr West of the Inner Temple a Secr of that Soc. shewd Them a Copy of King John's Magna Charta On Vellum, done from that preservd out of the Fire of the Cotton Library. by order of Lo High Chancellor & Speaker of the House of Comōns & Lo CJ of BR & al, & the Armes of the Noble Men, Trustees for Its Performance, emblazond in the Margin in Gold and proper Colours.

21 Junij The Reverd the Presidt in the Chair & Eight other Regular Members & Mr Lawrence an Honorary Member & Mr Calamy Joes permitted to be present

Microscopical Observations Mr Lawrence shewd the Soc. several Microscopical Observations with the Glasses belonging to the Soc. of the Circulation of the Blood in y Water Newt or Evet, & Some Minutes animals bred in Fluids

Coine of Didius Julianus the Secr. Lent the Treasurer a drawing of this rare medal in the Larger Brass of CÆSAR MARCVS DIDIVS SEVERVS IVLIANVS AVGVSTVS in y Collection of R Gale Esqr member of y Soc.

20

The Rev'd the President in the Chair & Tenn Othe Regular Members
& one honourary

The Secr acquainted the Soc. That James Theobald Esq: one of the Secr of thee Antiquarian Soc. & of the Councill of the Royal Soc. accepted their Invitation of becoming an honourary Member of this Soc. And he was declared a Member thereof accordingly

J. Theobald Esq: ab'd

That at the Royal Soc. 14 Inst: was read an Accurate description of the most uncom'on Fowles & plants in Carolina drawn painted and described by Mark Catesby there

Catesby of Carolina

& there was produced a Calculus humanus oblong as big as ones Fist voided by a Woman

Calculus

& read a paragraph of a L'r: from the Hague of a Cow lately killed there. 6 feet high, Eleven feet Long, weighing 2685 ℔.

Large Cow

D'r Lynn shewd the Soc. a Bridge for a Base Viol invented & made by him in Forme of the Rialto at Venice so contrived as to be capable of raising any or all the 4 Strings to what height you please by gently Skrewing up Spindles which elevate small peices of wood let into the Arch whereupon the Strings lye, being a very curious peice of Mechanisme, cleverly contriv'd

Bridge for Base Viol

John *Robert* Mitchell of London M.D. a Learned Physician was at his own Instance propos'd by M'r Johnson Jun'r: to be admitted a Member of this Society

D'r Rob't Mitchell opposed

Librarian to S'r R'd Ellys

The Rev'd the President in the Chair & Fourteen Other Regular Members And One Honourary Member

The Secr: brought in S'r Rich'd Ellys's Donation to the Library of this Soc. as a Regular & most beneficious Member thereof Bern'd Picard. Ceremonies & Costumes Religieuses de tous le peuple du Monde Representées par des Figures en Taille douce. 4 Vol's in Folio finely bound, for w'ch Noble & generous Benefaction the Soc. express'd themselves highly pleas'd & obliged.

S'r Richard Ellys Bar'tt's Donation

He also gave them an Impression of a large oval Seale whereon a prælate mitred his Right in a posture of Benediction, a cross in his left. & Layman suppose an Earle or Alderman with a Coronett on & a Battle Ax in his left hand, his right on his Breast in 2 Niches joyned a Top with pinacle work, on the Bishops, Abb'y or prelate side an Escutcheon Quarterly England & France semy de Lys. on the Earles Aldermans or Shireves side another of England only 3 Lyons passant guardant. underneath them between 2 large Flowers a Cheveron charged with 3 flower de Lys, a Croun or Coronett, a Lyon passant guard't & a Crosier as in the Margent

The Scale of y'e Abbey of Welho by Grymesby & Armes

the Inscription or Legend round the Seale

on the Back of the Seale

S:COE:ABBT:ET:OVENT:MOASTII:SCI:AVGVSTINI:DE:GRIMESBY.   #DnS:IohES:de:
Sigillum Commune Abbatis et Conventus Sancti   Vtterby: Xiiij:
AUGUSTINI de GRIMESBY.   Abbas:

Leland in Coll. Ect. IV. 93. Grymesby Monial Prior. [LINC.] Redditus annui X. li. Dugd. 9. 147.
Item. Wellow Abbat. Canon. Reg. or. S. Aug. prope ipsum op. de Grymesby,
Johannes Rex 1'r Fundator. in Confirm. R's H. 2. Dced Ecl. S'Aug. de Grymesby & Canonicis locum ubi =
Radulphus Filius Drogonis dedit maximam partem terræ. | = Sita est Abbatia qui dicitur Welhove
Annui redditus 152 li. | Dugd. 1 Mon. Angl. 1041. Welloo Abb. 95. 6. 1. |
Ecctia D. Jacobi de Grymesby appropriata.
Idem V. 2. 343 ex chron. Tho. franciscani ad Epsby. ait int al. sub fr'e W'o de Abyngdon — mutatus est locus de Grymesby.

This fine Seale is of Brass & was found in Glemesby th'n & is in the possession of Roger Gale Esq; a worthy Member of this Soc.

The Secr. at the desire of the Soc. of British Antiquaries in Londn. left in
English Gold Coines
B Willis
M Foulkes
this Soc. Claps over the chimney. A printed Table of the Gold Coines of ye
Kings of England compiled by Brown Willis Esquire a Member of ye
Soc. wch has a rich Collection of them, & whereof Martin Foulkes Esq, another
Member is about publishing an History, inviting all Members of this
to add to the sd Table an acct of wt They may have or have Seen &
where & of what Kings therein omitted, engaging to comunicate Such
Additions to the Ingenious Editor.

Dr Robert Mitchell of Londn. was put up again being proposd last Soc.

Antique Venus Victrix
an Impression of antique Gemme of B Bells Esq a Member representing a Female Fig
Venus Victrix holding an helmett in her right hand & a Dart in her left with ye
Elbow of wch She leans on a pastum of a shaft of a pillar agt wch is a Shield and
before her Stands a Boy holding up a Ferula.

Heraldry Peel
also another of a very large Modern Seal of the arms of Peel   a Lyon rampt
holding a Fish in his dexter paw Empaled with   a Bend Ermyne.

Gerves's Water Engine for Seats.
Mr Grundey a Member shewd the Soc. the Plan of Geo Gerves's Multiplying-
Wheel Bucket Engine for raising Water to Supply Gentlemens Seats
moving continualy by a Small Stream of Water, erected at Chichely
the Seat of Sr John Chester Bart in Bucks 1725 drawn by Mr
Henry Beighton F.R.S. engrav by E. Kirkall, with a printed Explanation thereof, wch Says ye Spring of Water wch feeds this Engine runs
four Gallons ⅌ Minute & is conveyd 72 Yards, the Engine in June 1727
Sr John Chester certified that it had gone very well from Its erection &
wanted no Repairs or Attendance more than giving the Iron Work a little
Oyle, & Supplyd his House and Offices with Plenty of Water and a Considerable Overplus for Fountains & other Convenient Uses.

Curious Watch made by Graham
Mr Lawrence a Member shewd the Soc. a Gold Watch made by Mr Graham (wo was
sometime partner with Tompion) the Movemts on Diamonds, & points without
bearing on Shoulderings, the wheels all parallell, & but 3 instead of 4.
the Scecond hand he can Stop & let go at the Space of half a Second. Cost 33 Gs
a very exact Automaton, & alt Varys not the motion by any Shakeing

12 July
The Revd the President in the Chair, and four other regular
Members.

Conven: tual. Ch. of Spalding
mm that in digging to lay the Foundation of Mr Operator Coxe's House next the Soc. Room
were dugg up several large Stone Coffins, & n pinacle Stone of one of the 3 Spires of the antient
Condentual th. 8 angular, wth a carved Cogg at each angle ⟨drawing⟩ after this Forme the front
there was an hole thro the middle to fix a Fane or Weather Cock in & it was cramped in front
several human Bones & Skulls were likewise found there.

Dr John Mitchell elected
Mr Hydes Donacon.
Dr John Mitchell of London was upon Ballott elected an Honorary
Member of the Society. B this Gent way Sr Ellys's Librarian
The Revd Mr Hyde Rector of Sutton sent his donation The London Cases of Controversial divinity, 3 Vols 5

22

The Revd the Presidt in the Chair, and Fourteen other Regular Members.

Mr Johnson a Secr of this Soc. shewd them a Curious Medal of the Middle Brass size & of that fine mettle comonly called Corinthian but not perfectly preserved having layn long in the head of Dunstan Spring about the Middle of Lincoln heath where It was taken up by some workmen employd by Edward Walpole Esq, Lord of that Mannor, when they cleared & opend the fountain head, and made a Cold Bath there, who gave It him. on the one side is the head of Antonia the Wife of Nero Cl. Drusus Germanicus the Mother of Germanicus Cæs. & Ti. Claudius afterwds Emper, wch then in honr of her caused It to be made of that Metal as Æn. Vico in his Augustarum Imagines p. 59 says.

Medal of Antonia Mater Claudij

Corinthian Brass.

ANTONIAE AVGVSTAE ½ an human Figure standing TI CLAVDIVS CAESAR AVG &c
on each side a Letter S. C. vide Oeconem p. 66. femina fuit honestissima & continentissima.

He also shewd ye Soc. the Original Instrumt of the Foundation of the Chantry of the holy Trinity in the Chapell of B.V.M. at Lowth in this County, endorsed Ordinacio Cantarie Thome de Luda in Ecclia de Luda. whereby he gives several houses & lands for maintainance of William de Setford a preist & his Successors to support the Service of prayers enjoyned wch begins Universis sancte mris ecclie filijs psentem Cartam inspris vel audituf Thomas de Luda Clavitus Lincoln salm in dno sempitnam. and ends His test dno Simone le chaumbleyn milite. Walto Rybaud, heruco, Walhesbe, heni de Stineton. Rogero Oibitt. & alijs. Dat apd Ludastio die mensis Aplis. Anno Dni millio cco septimo decimo, i.e. 3 Apr. 10 E.2. 1317.

Lowth Chantry

for the Souls of Wm the sd Founders Father, Margaret his Mother, his Bretheren & all his Benefactors, every day at the Altar of the sd Holy Trinity, to hold to the sd Chaplain & his Successors in puere & ppetual Almes for their Sustenance, 5 Collects tobe said in the Mass so appoynted One for the Founders health of his body & soul whiles living & when dead for his Soul, the 2d for the Souls of his Father & Mother, 3d for his Bretheren 4th for his Spiral Benefactors, 5 for all Faithfull living or Dead. except on certain Festivals therein mencond when certain Offices are appoynted in lieu thereof, expresly ordaining and enjoyning the Chaplain not to wast or indiscreetly dispose of any thing so settled or given for the Support of himself & his proper Ch, at least not of the Chalice, Books, Vestments & other Ornaments requisit to the sd Chantry which the sd Founder had provided & wch the Chaplains for the time to come were to minister repaire & preserve. So that neither the Rector of the Mother Ch, nor Vicar, &c should have power over the goods &c of the sd Chantry nor the Chaplain to devise them or the profits thereof unreceived by his Will. The Chaplain to assist at divine Service in the sd Ch. of Lowth, particularly in Singing, on death cession or amotion the profits to be reserved for the Successor, in Sickness to take Care the duty bedone by some Deputy. Every New Chaplain to be Sworn to Observe these Ordinances & after the Founders decease to come in by Collation of the Ld Bp of Lincoln there's a Salvo iure ipsius ecclie pbendal de Luda &c. inserted here and there.

the Designe of Chantrys

And just before the Close are the Formes of the 5 Collects above enjoined as prescribed tobe said by the Chantry Priest. I have made the abstract of the Foundation of this Chantry fuller to shew the Nature and designe of such sort of Charities which were dissolvd as superstitious by the Statutes 37 H.8. & 1 Ed.6. Cap.14. and were so Comon that there was hardly a Church in England without such a foundation in It. Now to give some Acct of the Founder. I find that 1310 he was constituted Prebend of Sexaginta Solidorum in the Cath Ch. of B.V.M. at Lincoln, wch he quitted for that of Welton Paynshall in the same Ch. 1312 & that for Marston St Lawrence there 1315. wch he left the Yeare after being collated to yt of Langford Mannor 23d of June. 1321. he was Instituted Treasurer of the sd Cathedral and died 1329. as appeares by the Probate of his Will in April that yeare.

& Revd Thomas of Lowth

v. Brown Willis Surv. of Linc Cath. p. 93. 199. 214. 237. 260.

Lowth Preb &c

The Prebend of Lowth hath his Title from a Prebendary in the sd Cath Ch. So named of Lowth a great Markett Town in Lincolnsh. where the prebendary has as I judge (says Willis p. 212.) the Tythes and Advowson & about the time of the foundation of this Chantery therein Wm de Melton the Prebendary thereof was made Arch Bishop of York & succeeded in his Prebend by Goceline Cardinalis. Lowth was given to the Cath Ch. of Lincoln by W.1. as seems by his Son W.2. Censrus 3 Mon. 260. Pat. 8. H.6. p32. m. 10. & the Bull of Pope Honorius dat. 1125. ibm 269.

Cure for the Eyes by Causticks

The Presid[t] com[d] to the Soc. an History of an Extraordinary Cure [y]found by M[r] Belon Surjeon Maj[r] to the King of France at the Hospital of Briancon 1691. upon a Soldier who had the Ball of one of his Eyes entirely consumed by a Semicircle of the Caustick Stone lay[d] on behind each Eare, w[ch] he affirms he practiced on Others with great Success and that M[r] Calcau a Master Surjeon at Turin thereby cured a Prie[st] of a Gutta Serena – refers to 2[d] Vol of the Hospital Surjeon by Belon.

Linseed oyl

He also Shew[d] [y]e Soc. a Skin taken off of a Pot of Lineseed Oyl very beautyfull, of a Gold colour

M[r] Taylor ppos[d]

John Taylor M.A. Fellow of S[t] John's Coll. in Cambridge & deputy Librarian of the University Library was at his own Instance propos[d] by the Rev[d] M[r] Ray to be admitted a Member of this Society

26. July The Rev[d] the President in the Chair & Thirteen other Regular Members

Oxon Terræfilius L[r]. from M[r] Johnson [&] M[r] Falkner

Secr com[d] to y[e] Soc. part of a L[r] from M[r] Rich[d] Falkner of Lincoln Coll Oxford to him wherein that Ingenious young Gent kindly promises to send him drawings and accounts of any thing he desires from the Museum Ashmoleanum &c wch L[r] was sealed with an elegant Impression of a Female Busto. and as an Earnest thereof he read the Intended P[er]formance of y[e] Terræfilius for this late Act, sent last post by that Correspondent.

Deed of Exch[g] between a Gentleman & y[e] Convent of Gerondon in Leicestersh[r] dat[ed] in 1455

The s[d] Secr also Shew[d] the Soc. an Ind[re] very finely written on Velom beginning
Hec indentura facta int[er] Joh[em] Trenthall de Westloughton in Com[e] Lincoln Armigerum ex [una] parte [&] Abbatem Monasti[i] Beate Marie de Gerondon ejusdem loci Conventus ex parte alt[era]
being an Exchange made between y[m] 2 several Fourscore acres of land & pasture in Cortlyngstoke in the County of Nottingham with mutual Covenants for the Enclosing & quiet Enjoym[t] that each party might a[s]sartare, includere cum Sepibus Fossatis vel muris & hold the p[re]misses in Severalty and with reciprocal warranty of Them so enclos[d] contra omnes Gentes Under the seal of the [sd] J Trenthall, & the Comon Seal of the [sd] Abley & Conv[t] Alternatim. hijs Testibus Thoma Staunton de Sutton juxta Bovyngton Joh[e] Brokesby de Frysby Hugone Annesley de Rodyngton Armigeris Thoma Farnham de Querndon Gentilman Rob[to] Farnham de ead[em] Gentilman W[o] Bowes de Cortlyngstoke Gentilman W[o] Pegg de Loughtburgh Gentilman & multis alijs Dat[um] in domo Capitulari de Gerondon 8[o] die April A[o] hij[us] R[s] Henrici Sexti post Conquest[um] Anglie 33 [ie 1455] this Abbey is in Leycest[ersh]r & was found[d] by E[rl] Rob[t]. A[o] Dni 1133. & 4 bovat or Ox gang. menconed to be been given to It in Cortlyngstoke by Willm de Bones in the Confirm Cart in Ed. 3. N. 17 [&] Inspex. Dugd. Monastic Anglic. 768. fol. – Robert Beaumont, de Bello Monte Sirnamed Bossu Earle of Leycester was y[e] Founder

M[r] Taylor of S[t] Johns was put up again being propos[d] last Society.

2[d] August
D[r] Lynn V.P. in the Chair, & ~~Nine~~ Ten other Members whereof Nine Regular and the Rev[d]. M[r] John Rowney M.A. Fellow of Magdalen Coll. Cambr. & M[r] Townshend [ad]mitted to be present.

L[d] Trevor Epitaph.

Read the Epitaph put upon the Monum[t] of y[e] late W[orshipfu]ble Tho. Lord Trevor at Bromham Sometime Sollicitor then Attorney General afterw[d] D.C.I. B.C. made Peer by Q Ann – [Ld] privy Seal by K.G.1. and president of [y]e Councill by his present Majesty.

Experim[t] of Juices of Herbs for Staining Paper

The Secr Shew[d] the Soc. y[e] Effect of the Experiments of Staining according to the hon[ble] M[r] Robert Boyles one[s] method wth Alom & G[u]mm Water published & practiced 17 August last with these Herbs, Fruits, & Flowers [vizt] Cyanus Cæruleus or Blew fields Bottle, purple Holyoake, Indian Figg, Strawbery Spinag[e], Papaver rheas red field Poppy, House leek, Dandalyon, Marygold flower, Vine Leaves, Eldren leaves, Tanasy, Som[e] or Sow thistle, Tithymal or Spurge, Stramonium or Thorne apple – of which three [1] Cyanus, Stramonium & purple Holyoake best answer expectation the first yielding as fine a Blew as Ultramarine the 2[d] an Agreeable yellowish Green, the last a deep purple. M[r] B. Bell says the Imp[re]ss[ed] Juices on his Tryals succeeded not so well as these.

Mr Johnson Secr. read to the Soc. Some Acct of the learned Robt Wakefield and his Oration shewing the Usefullness of the Oriental Languages, 1524. & of the first Oriental Types. at the Instance of the Revd Mr Ray and for the use of his Frs &c. Mr Tegg SIGSS.

He also shewd ye Soc. a fine Print of Melbord Castle in Derbyshire formerly a Royal Mansion, where John Duke of Bourbon great Chamberlain and General of the French taken prisoner by the invincible K9 H.V in the Battle of Agincourt 1414 was kept prisoner several Years, lately belonging to Mr Vice Chamberlayne Coke

And another of Tutbury Castle in Staffordshire built abt the Conquest both engraven from Original Drawings in the Dutchy office with leave of the most Noble the Dk of Rutland Chanceller, by George Vertue SA & GSS Sculpt SA. Londini. 1733.

also Mr Chambers's Considerations for Enlarging his Cyclopædia or Dictionary, by rendering It much more general in a Second Edition, ye former having been greatly Approved by the Publick & purchasd by this Soc. for their Publick Library.

also a Sea Horse, or small dryd Fish in this Shape & size caught by Captn Thomas in the Bay of Biscay the Horse-Fish. Hippocampus. a Small Fish, so called because its head is Shaped like an Horses and his Taile divided by, several Incisures, somewt like those of Caterpillars ΚΑΜΠΑΙ Vide Grews Mus Reg Soc. fo: 101.

Mr John Taylor MA. Fellow of St Johns Coll Cambr & deputy Library of that University was upon Ballott admitted a Member of this Society

The Revd the President in the Chair and Twelve Other Regular Members And the Revd Mr Rewney of Magdalen Coll Cambr present

Mr Johnson Secr read to the Soc. a Lr to him from Beaupré Bell Esq of Trin Coll Cambr dated from Beaupré Hall Norf. 2 Inst. shewing the Method by which that learned and Ingenious Member of this Soc. proposes to determine what Medals or Coines have been stamped, & what Cast by the Hydrostatic Ballance, to distinguish Counterfiet Cast speices that way from the genuine Originals Stamped or Hammerd: which were which being as he says as yet onely an Hypothesis, I forbear to give a summary of he not having not had Opportunity of makeing due Experiments, tho he's well satisfyd, from some such Sort of Hydrostatical Experiments he made when here the later End of last Month with Dr Lynn & the Secr of some Coines & Medals in the sd Secr. Collectn, and his Other Observations on the Nature and weight of Metal that a Standard may be found to determine this point by, which is a Consideration entirely New and by him added to all the Others from Vaillant, Spanheim, Banduri, Walker, Jobert &c in a Summary at the End of his intended preface to his Tabulæ Augustæ, of wch the plan & proposals were communicated to this Soc. 19 Octr last, And which many of the Members have promoted by Subscriptions & Communicating what they've observed may best tend towd the speeding that noble Designe.

also a Copy of Verses spoken at the last Oxford Act upon the Hippo or Vapours entitled in a Lr to him from Mr Falkner of Lincoln Coll. Oxf. which that Ingenious Young Gent supposes may the more Acceptable as he hears they're not to be printed, tho well worthy of the press, giving a Just representation of the dire Effects of that sad Distemper in very elegant Latin and with a true poetick Spirit.

Mr B Bell lent the Soc. for farther Improveing their Collections towds a Grand & General of Arts & Sciences a long thin pap. MSS. entitled Literarum Nexus, ex MSS. collegit Beauprens Bell. M.D.CC.XXIX. ⚹ & presented ye 16th Casts of Eight Arabick or Turkish Scales, Persian

MS.
Abbre-
viatures.
B Bell.
sept. 16.
Plagix

Which worthy and Industrious Member sometime since also lent us for carrying on or so grand Designe of the Alphabet of Arts and Sciences another MS. Collection made by him Entitled – E Codice MS. contin. M. T. Ciceronis Opera Philosophica exarato A.D. 1444. taken as These now communicated with great labour & exactness ∴ 7 November 1734, these MSS entred & returned ∴ Also for the farther promoting our said Work presented the Soc. now with a small printed Book Entitled Repertorium Sculptile Typicum, Or a complete Collection & Explanation of the several Marks & Cyphers By w᷄ ye Prints of the best Engravers are distinguished, with an Alphabetical Index of their Names, places of abode, & times, in w᷄ they lived translated from the ABCEDARIO PITTORICO of Pellegrini Antonio Orlandi, as I have heard by Rich᷄ Middleton Massey M.D. of the Royal Antiquarian & this Soc. printed at Lond᷄ 1736. in 12º / Mr Rowland a worthy Memb᷄ undertook to transcribe ye.

Lr from
Mr H Johnson

Sevilla
Hispalis

Vast
Brick
Tower

Italica

Amphi.
-theatre

City of
Sevill

& church.

The d᷄ Secr also read greatest part of a very long Lr dated from Sevilla in Spain June 2᷄ OS. to him from his Kinsman Henry Johnson Esq a worthy learned and Ingenious Member of ye and the Antiquarian Soc. Giving an Ample description of the City of Sevill the Aquæduct. Temples, & other Buildings and Antiquities there particularly a Collection of Antique Statues in the Palace of the Marquis de Priego one of the first Grandees of Spain, both ye Ornam᷄ & Ex of the Moorish Brick Tour (phaps says he the noblest brick building in the World, Its heighth as built by the Moors is 250 Spanish feet, on w᷄ the Spaniards have erected another structure 100 feet higher, So that now Its whole height from the Ground is 350 feet Spanish, what is most remarkable in It is the Ascent on the Inside which is one continual plain without steps from Bottom to Top so broad that 2 Horsemen abreast with Lances in their hands may ride up to Its heighth and down again with Ease – this is the Reverse of all other Buildings in the World for tho Higher one ascends the Walls thereof are found still to encrease in thickness: then follows some Acc᷄ of Italica formerly a Roman Municipium now a heap of ruins about a League to the Eastward from Sevill And of the ruines of an Ampitheatre there, a plan whereof he says he see in the possession of Mr Keen the British plenipotentiary at the Court of Spain It was in length 160 Spanish Vares

in Breadth 140

Its area 85 by 65

And Its heighth 25 Vares

Then he proceeds to give some Acc᷄ of the King and his Court & palace, formerly the Royal Alcazar of a Moorish King

Then of the City of Sevill he says the Walls are 5½ Miles in Circumference within are no more than 29 parishes and yet there are 118 Churches (vizt 29 Parish Churches. 45 Convents of Fryers 28 of Nuns 16 Hospitals adding to these the Churches & Chappells of the Suburbs they are in all 220.

Here

Here too is the tremendous Clenk of the Inquisition, wch was formerly an Old Moorish Castle or palace, there are in this Town upwards of 4000 Officers which belong to It

The Inquisition

The Cathedral Church of Sevill is a Vast disproporcond Gotlick Building 420 Spanish feet in Length 263 in Breadth 126 in heighth - 5 naves the Pillars 14 Vares in Circumference In't 83 Chapells & Altars and there are at less 500 Masses ø diem Sung in It It has an ArchBishop 14 Dignitarys Each of wch on Solemn Festivals weare a Mitre, of wch the Deane is Chief. 40 Cannons & 60 Praebends theRent of the Bp are 120 000 Ducats Yearely. the Dean has C000, the Canons 30 000 Rials each besides an Annual Rent of 40 000 Ducats fo Fabrick Money

The Cathedral
Dignitary
Revenues

Amongst these Treasures is a Vast large Coffin of Massy Silver and most Curious Workmanship in which is preserved the Body of San Ferdinand the King who conquerd this City from the Moors, & which in a Most Solemn manner is exposd to publick View twice a Yeare. this Prince succeeded K H. 1216 & dyed 1252.

Silver Shrine of St Ferdinand

The learned Writer says Ilispalis was a Roman Colony & favourite City of Julius Cæsar wch may be called a 2^d Founder of It, he enlarging Its privileges & calling It after his own Name IVLIA ROMVLA. as by many latin Inscriptions on Marble may be Seen, tho most of them are broken and defaced, in the Corners & sides of every Street are seen most Beauty full peices of Marble Pillars, so round the CAthedral, half-buryd under ground & serving only as posts to keep off Carryages

Remains of Roman Antiquities at Sevill
Columnes

The God who formerly was chief in the devotion of this place was the Libean Hercules, who once had a noble Temple here some Ruins may be still traced out as it took up in extent a whole Parish (now called of San Nicholas) two of Its Pillars wch I imagine to have been of its Portico they have erected, wch by the Eye I judge to be ab^t 70 feet in height - all of one piece in Marble of the Corinthean Order; Their Circumference equall to y^ height, these stand at the entrance of a long Walk, like our Mall in St James's Park, on the top of one is a large Statue of Julius Cæsar, on the other a Hercules, both of them inclining on large Shields on which are cut the present Arm's of Spain, wch these poor People believe to be of equal date with the Pillars! these were discovered under Ground with 4 others of the same Size in the spott where the Antient Temple was believed to be, the other 4 remain buried still. beside these I have seen two more wch by their Size I imagine to be full as big as the forementioned but there appears no more of them above ground than about one Yard and an half these 2 the people say are placed here in remembrance of Julius Cæsar, & they are just by two old Roman Arches which though joyned together jet stand Angular fashion, wch I imagine must be part of some ancient Temple, perhaps of Bacchus who was also particularly worshipped here, tho: there is no body that can give any certain account of them.

Temple of Libyan Hercules
2 Vast Corin Columnes
Colossean statues of J. Cæsar & Hercules
Temple of Bacchus

Dr Lynn a Member of this Soc. read a Discourse of his own concerning his intended Treatise upon the Small Pox. the Usefullness of Mechanismes & Art of Swimming. which he took away with him.

Dr Lynn

On the Proposal of several Regular Members the following Noblemen & Gentlemen were
proposd to be invited as Usual to become Members of this Society. And to be Actualy so,
NB. Upon Notification of their Acceptance. S.r Hans Sloane Bar.t R.S.P. & Coll Med.Pr.

The R.t Re.d D.r Tho. Tanner L.d Bishop of St. Asaph S.T.P. FAS.

×Edward× Alexander of Dr.s Comons Esq. LLB. Accepted

David Atkinson of Lincolns Inn & Fanthorp by Louth Esq.

R.t Hon.ble Rich.d Boyle Earle of Burlington

Mons.r Le Blon of Little Chelsea Park Painter & Tapistry Weaver

Dixon Coleby of Stanford MD.

R.t Hon.ble Scott Earle of Dalkeith

Robert Darwin of Lincolns Inn & Elston Nott. Esq.

S.r Jermyn× Davers of Rushbrook Bar.tt Kn.t of y.e Shire for Suffolk accepted

S.r John Evelyn of Bar.t VP.AS & FRS.

S.r Andrew Fountain of Kn.t her Maj.tie VC. FAS.

R.t Hon.ble Maurice Thompson Lord Haversham Baron of Haversham

Jones Musick Master

His Excellency Coll.t Rob.t Johnson Governour of South Carolina

James Joye of Bennyfield North.t Esq.

W. Kent of Painter

Rev.d Charles Lamotte D.D. FR.&A.S

×Carteret× Leethes of Accepted Esq. Memb.r of Part. for

Smart× Lethieullier of accepted Esq.

Rev.d Roger Long D.D. Rector of Orton North.t FRS

Mr Lynnwood Merchant at Oporto

S.r George Markham of Bar.tt FRS.× accepted

R.t Hon.ble Clinton Earle of Lincoln FAS.

Mr Tho Martin of

S.r Mich.l Newton of Bar.t & Kn.t of the Bath Burgess for Grantham

×Robert ×New of the Middle Temple Esq. FAS. accepted

Mr Rich.d Norcliffe Merch.t at Frederickshall in Norway

×John ×Ravenscroft of Wyrtham by Spalding & Liffenham Esq. accepted

Mr Reysbraeck of Statuary & Sculptor

Mr Stranovius an Hungarian Gent & Painter at Vienna

Rev.d Tookie DD.

S.r James Thornehill of Kn.t his Maj. Painter & Burg. fo.

×Edward Walpole× of Dunstan on Lind Heath Esq. accepted

Wallis of Stanford MD.

Dymoke of Boston MD.

Hon.ble Wentworth of Lillingston Lovell Bucks. Esq.

Rev.d Bernard Willson M.A. Vic.r of Newark up. Trent & Preb. of Linc.

16.th Aug. The Rev.d the Pres.d in y.e Chair & Five Other Regular Members pre.t
1733 The Proposal for Inviting all the several Noblemen & Gent. above mentioned & their respec-
Invitat.o tive Names being severaly read over aloud was Balloted & Order.d y.t They be Invited accordingly

28

Mr Johnson Secr. commund to the Soc. part of a Lr to him from Wm Bogdani Esq a Member
dated from the Tower of Londn 9 Inst. wherein he gives a drawing and Acct of a Medal in
the large Brass in his poss TI. CAESAR. AVGVSTI. F. IMPERATOR V   4 allare ROME ET AVG.

Also another from Gr Lynn Inr another Member datd fram Southwick 13 Inst. giving
some Acct of the New Organ Set up in the Great Ch. at Coventry

Mr Bells reet for makeing red Ink — Boile the Shaveings of Brazile Wood in
Vinegar (with a little Tartar & allam) till It comes to the Colour you like,
then Strain It and add a little Gumm Arabick.

The Word ΗΡΟΣ sometimes otherwise spelld, is found sometimes on Greek, Ægyptian
& Roman Coines or Medals, more frequently on Antique Gemms or Intaglias.
It generaly precedes the Parties proper Name, ΗΡΟΣ ΑΝΤΟΟΣ Du Choul. 231.
ΗΡΑΣ ΕΥΡΥΠΥΛΟΣ in Haverchamp's pref. to Josephus 2 pref. fo v7. from Spanheim.

tho Sometime It follows the parties proper name, as ΑΝΤΙΝΟΟΣ ΗΡΟΣ. Du Choul ubi Supr
tis Sometimes written or Spelld as ΕΡΩΣ with an Ω as that preceding Eurypylus
Seems rather an Ω than an Ο. the Forme plainly & widely differing from the Ö in
his Name as above written, And in an Intaglia belonging to the Secr. Mr Johnson
know Shewn the Soc. whereon is cut a Very beauty full head of a Youth —
Just before & parallell allmost with the Outline of his Head is this Inscription

ΕΡΩC· ΕΒ· ΟΡ Α

in Sigillo Amethystino penes Mauritium Johnsonll. SRS Secr. ex donis Dni. Gerardi operis
Græcanici eximij, forsan Caput Getæ Cæsario & legendum Herois Eboracensis.

And it is rightfully enough thus written ΕΡΩΣ ab ἑραῶ amo, Seu ΗΡΣΩ απο
Τῦ ΕΡΩΤΟ virtutis Studio, Seu Amore hominum quem sibi virtutis Amor
conciliaberat, & So comes to the Same Sense. Hence the brave Youth had
the Appellation of HEROES, and hence wee read of their Heroick exploits
Mons. Jobert (in his Science de Medailles, says he has Seen Some of Antinous
with ΗΡΟC, ΗΡΣΩ & ΗΡΩΟΣ. but attributes the last to a Mistake of Mintmaster. p. 519.
Hence Herus became a Complimentary Title, with the Latins, & hepe man with
the Saxons. with whom hepe simply signified an Armed force or Military Power,
from them the Germans use heretog and heertogh for a General Teuton. hertzog
for a Sovereigne Lord Duke zoza AS. Dux; So on the Silver Coines of the House
of Brunswick AUGUSTUS HERTZOG ZU BRAUNS: UND L: ALLES MIT BEDACHT. 1642.
Instead of Sr. Mr or Mons myn Heer is the modern Appellation of a Dutch man
addressing him Self to any Gentleman

I won't omitt that Our Escuage, Scutagium a Duty formerly paid or levyd according
to Knights Fees in our old Military Tenure was called Sometimes hereschildt, I
think rather as It was a Shield or Defence of the Lord for preserving his possesion,
than as Some have thought quasi Exercitūs Scutum.

The D Secr. likewise Shewd ym a curious Petrifaction of an Ostracites or rather of
a flatt Cockel half next the Shell transparently Christallizd, the other half ragg
Mr Operator Cox Sayd he had observed Such Petrifactions as these lay in the
Stoney Matter or Earth & the Christallized Side is alway undermost
And he attributes that part being Christallized the more to the Salts of the
Substance of the Fish and Its juices So Subsiding & lying downeward.

23 Aug.ᵗ The Rev.ᵈ ỹ Presidᵗ in ỹ Chair, & Eleven Other regular Members

Cast — Mʳ Mercer a Member presented the Musæum with an Octangular Cast, on one side Sᵗ Joseph, holding the Blessed Child Jesus in his left Arm & supported on his right a Bṗ in his Pontificals laying his right hand on a Woman kneeling, with a Nimbus round her head, a Man behind holding his Crosier. B.TVRRIB·ARCH·LIM. very fine work.

Honorary Members — The Secr Mʳ Johnson Notified to the Soc. That Edward Alexander Esq. Sʳ George Markham Barᵗ, Mʳ Tho. Marten, Robert New Esq, & Edward Walpole of Dunstan Esq, had accepted their kind Invitation to become Members of this Soc. Captⁿ Pilliod also Notified to the Soc That Carteret Leethes Esq, had accepted of the same the Treasurer also notified to the Soc That Sʳ Germin Davers Baronᵗ and John Ravenscroft Esq, had accepted of the Same, & they were all Accordingly declared Honorary Members of this Society.

Golden Chalices — Mʳ Butters a Member ẅ has lately been at York acquaint the Soc by the sᵈ Secr. ỹ he was Shewn in the Cathedral of ỹ City 2 Golden Chalices with 2 patens of ỹ Same Metal lately dug up out of the Grave of an ABṗ of that Province buryd there abᵗ 300 Yeares agone

Gigantic Muscle Concha Tridachna Exotica — Sᵗ Mʳ Johnson Secr presented the Musæum with a Great Waved Muscle Shell Nineteen Inches long & 5½ over in the widest part, Phaps the Cocha Maxima marmorea Exotica imbricata of Columna — described by Grew Mus Reg Soc. 147. but lest by a ỹ this It was taken by Captⁿ Thomas not far from Smyrna, It's calld Pinna or Asturaby = Matthiolus or dioscorides fol. 200.

Xtalizd Pebble — Also a white Peble very curiously Christalisede.

Tripos — Mʳ Rowland a Member shewd ỹ Soc. a Tripos Speech in Print sayd to be made for ỹ Oxfʳᵈ act

a Riddle on the Letter H — a Riddle in Verse composed by that Ingenious Lady Mʳˢ Willis of Exton

In a List of Old Worthys I stand high in Fame
Whilest of Me but Seven præcedency claim
In mighty Atchievements I still bear a part
& every Monarch has me at his Heart:
In Holland Im first; am much in ỹ Church,
& Yet by all Parties am left in ỹ Lurch.
Was oft us'd in old Athens, am there now not known,
From Politeness alike, and Barbarity flown:
In Hurry & Mischief I allwaies appeare,
Yet neer Stir from Home, nor out my Chair
Tho' 'bove a Thousand Yeares old yet this is a Truth
Im allways in Health, & allways in Youth,
And So long agoe for thos: who gave Laws
To th' World, I began their complimentary clause.
Nor saluted the Living alone, but the Dead;
As They very well know, who are very well read

a Tale in verse — Also a witty Poem of the Same Ladies in the manner of Fontaine, called a Tale on Ale, occasiond by a Villager & his Wife tapping before ỹ Feast.

30

Mr Johnson Senr comd a Copy of Verses from a Lady in France to Mrs Willes of Exton Rutland   **Epistolary Poems**
in return for a present of a Needleworked Carpett — in ye Epistolary way — to Mrs Willes's aunt,
both very Ingenious, and much after the manner of ye great Poet Mich Drayton.

Mr Johnson Secr shewd the Societie 2 Medals or Coines of Pompey the Great   **Medals**
one of the large Brass, with his head on one side, wth short Curld Hair & Beard **CN POMPEIVS MAGNVS**   Pompeius M
upon his Conquest of Mauritania so Syrnamed by Sylla 80 yeares before the Birth of our Saviour   Æ I
& a Rotonda wth Statues thereon & before It a portico & Columns wth a pediment over It. **COS III** underneath **CONSECRATIO**
yphaps this building is intended for the Theatre he built in or after his 3d Consulship according to Plutarch, which
was without a Collegue In the 701 yeare of the City, 51 yeares before Xt. Golts Fasti 176 to:

The other of Silver of the Denarius size the same head between a praefericulum & the augural crooked Staff   **Æ**
MAG·PIVS·IMPITER·TR on the 4 wch is somewt concave are 3 Mauls figures. He in the middst rests his right foot on the prow
of a Shipp & holds an Axe ἅγκυρα, or Amplustre or Naval Banner in his right hand, & an helme in his Left,
thore on each syde are as Occo will have the figure of Amphinomus & his bro. wth piety saved their parents from
the fury of Mount Ætna, a Type of piety proper to his new additional name of **PIVS** vide Vigilij Ætnam
in Oxurg **CLAS·ET·ORAE / MARIT·EX·S·C**   66 yeares before Xt. Golts Fasti 175. fol: Occo pagg 2. 3.

This was certainly struck in honour of his Great Conquests over the Cilician Pyrates who had gotten the whole
Mediterranean Sea into their power, for wch he was not only constituted Admiral & sole General at Sea of the
Romans, but by the Gabinian Law had absolute authority given him over all the Sea & maine land too for the
Space of 400 furlongs from the Sea   from Hercules pillars which warr plutarch repre-
Sents as very hazardous & of the highest Consequence to the Romans, and to be been soon ended by Pompey,
in wth Countenance rough strength & Hardyness, noted in him & Alexander the Great by Plutarch & Spon,
wch cites him for this in his 24 Dipos De lutilité des Medailles pour l'étude de la Phisionomie. p 360. 361.

On these Coines and 2 other small brass, one whereof British. a Venerable head of the great Cassivelaun.   **Æ**
wth short hair and long beard. ye concave an Horse & Wheel or Essedum wth **SAS** under the Horse. Cotempo- concave
rary with Pompey. the sd Secr. observed, that in all Metals Coines or Small Medals both
of the Britains & Romans had been struck **convexo capite**, unde 4 concavus fiebat.

And that untill the times of the Caesars the truly great Men were not so effeminately Curious   **Heroes intons**
about their Hair, hence in the Augustan times & after for reprehension of Coxcombs Horace
& other poets commend the **Intonsi Catones**: Lucan says of Pompeys Head **illa verenda**
Regibus hirta Coma, & generosa Fronte decora, Caesaries — & Silius Italicus in Imitation
of him - **Ille hirtâ cui subrigitur coma fronte, decorum.**   Epigramm terris **Magnus caput**

The Revd Mr Brainsby a Member presented the Museum with a large Cameleon, with   **Cameleon**
Several Eggs, brought from the Mediterranean

Dr Green a Secr of this Soc. presented ye Museum wth a peice of an Oake Pile taken up   Dutch Pile eat by
out of the Texel at the Sluice in Amsterdam much eaten by wormes when under   **Worms in ye**
Water after having been driven down but abt 9 months, ye Worms dy as soon as taken   Water.
out of the Water, the Wood unknawn appeares to be very firme.

The revd Mr Brainsby being become Rector of Great Cotes by Grimesby desired to   Revd Mr Brainsby
Continue an Honourary Member of this Soc. and on his declaring agreed to, he —   an honourary
having left the Parish of wch he was late Lecturer & Deputy Librarian of this Soc.   Member
in which Offices the Revd Mr Walter Johnson BTh succeeds him.

@Mr Brainsby promised the Soc. to continue a good Corresponding Member, &   **Gryme & Havelock**
was desired by the Secr to send us wth Information he could abt Grymd and Havelock of Grymesby.

Mr Pinche shewd the Soc. a peble transparent and prettily veined & clouded wth ben a good   **Polished Peble**
polish found at Harrow on the Hill, many such are found in Great Britain like fine Agates.

He promised very kindly of his own Accord to send the Soc. some things Curious   **Druggs**
in his way for improving their Museum

Twas desired to send the Oparator Mr Cox 6 Quart 6 pint & a doz less siz'd Cylindrical   **Glasses**
Long Clear Glass bottles for keeping Animals & Fœtus's in Spiritts, wch he kindly   for keeping
undertook to do.   Animals in

The Revd Mr Neve a Member by ye Secretary Mr — informd ye Soc. yt there hath been a Mosaich Pavemt
of Opus Tessellatum lately discovered at Chasterton in Flemington st, whereof he was shewd a dice or cube.

The Revd Mr Johnson LLB. VP. and Eight other Regular Members ———

1733

An Act of the Rebuilding Magdalen Coll in Oxford undertaken as good & begun this Month

Lr from Dr Falkner
Poetry on ye Oratorio

The Treasurer comend to the Soc. a Latin Poem which spoken upon Mr Hendel's Oratorio at ye Late Oxford Act which he recd in a Lr last post from Mr Falkner of Lincoln Coll: being an Alchaick Ode on the Triumph of Barach & Debora

Christalline Humour

Pupill of a Whales Eye

The Seer brought in the pupill of the Eye of a Whale upward of 80 feet long taken in the Greenland Fishery 3 years agone & presented to the Museum (as he has ever since kept it) by Captain Thomas. It is of a Transperent and pale Yellow of the Size & shape of a Roumceval Pea, & has a thin Sort of Filme or skin a little bloody on Some part of It, and shewd them a neat Print representing the manner of the Greenland Whale Fishery.

Deed of Remiss or Release without any Attestation but ye Seales

Mr Johnson ye Seer: shewd the Soc. a Deed Poll on Vellom beginning thus Noverint universi &c Psentes nos Willm Pynchbeck de Covyngton & Petrus Leke de Wrangle remisisse &c whereby for Themselves & their heires They released & quit claimed Dno Johi Peirson de Covyngton & Dno John Holdi &c all their Right & Title to ... unto place ... &c tuis in Covyngton &c They lately had together with Dame Margaret Wake late of Boston & Sr Tho Lawys late of the Same &c or by the demise & delivery of Wm Wright of Benyngton Junr & John Wright late Rectr of the Moyety of the Church of Leverton ... To have & hold to the sd John Peirson his heires & assigns ... In cuius rei testimom psentibz Sigilla nra apposuimus. Dat buoiaimo Septo dio Octobrio Anno Regni Regis Henrici Septimi post conquestu Anglie Duodecimo — AD. 1497·

Seales alone for Attestacon

What is very remarkeable in this Deed is That there is no manner of Attestacon thereto but barely the Seales of the parties Releffors appending by Labells of the like Vellom: the Impressions are Both of a Course red wax, Mr Pynchbecks, the Virgin Mary Sitting to the knees with the Child in her Armes; Mr Lekes defaced — It should Seem abt this time The Practicers began to omit the Clause Hijs Testibus— and Yet the parties did not as then Write their Names; Nor are there the Names of any Witnesses thereunto & happe it might be executed on the Pmisses, for sometimes otherwise It was not unusual to do It p Virgam, Fustem, aut Baculum v. major difsert ante Formulare Angl. fo. XIX.
These Deeds Poll were comonly in the first pson and began usualy, wth Omnibus Christi Fidelibus &c or sciant presentes & futuri &c but this begins like a Comon Bond vid: Litt. L.III § 372.

Lr from Mr Foe
Pot of Rom Coines found at Haynton

The sd Seer comd to ye Soc. ye Contents of a Lr to him from Mr Edd Foe a Curious pson in his Inquiryes dated at Horne Castle in ys County yesterday ye 5 Inst acquainting him that abt 14 days Since at the Seat of — Heneage Esq ffas Haynton in ys County 8 miles from Louth & 12 from Lincoln were found in digging to lay the foundation of a Dog Kennell a large Posnet Pot of old Roman Coines of different Sorts and Sizes The pot had 3 feet & an handle — the Value of the Silver comes to 40lb. Mr Heneage gave ye man wo found It 10 Guineas. Mr Foe adds there is an Old Roman Road that goes from Lincoln City wch he has travailed, and It points towards Haynton:

Lr from B Bell privy marks on Coines

The sd Seer also comund to the Soc. part of a Lr to him from Beaupré Bell Junr Esqr a Member dated from Beaupré Hall in Norff. 3 Aug Septr Inst. with the an Acct of such privy markes on English Gold & English Coines. 2 Eliz. KJ 1. & KJ C.1.

Cast of Seneca

He also shewd them a full faced Cast from an Antique of a Busto of SENECA the Philosopher

Mr Pincke proposed

Mr Edward Pincke of Ludgate Street Londn Druggist a very Eminent Dealer was proposed At his own Instance by Mr Jackson to be admitted an honourary Member of this Society

Francis Scott a Gent of Antwerp in his *Itinerario d'Italia* Parte 1. p 100.101. speaking of y. Church delle Gratie in Milan gives this Epitaph on the Beatrice the Lady of Lewis Sforza w. died in Childbed

V English Travailes thro Italy 1547 printed 1561. p 198 w. Gabriel Harveys Mss. Notes herein

Infœlix partus, amissa ante vita, quàm in lucem ederet,
Infœlicior, quod MAtri moriens vitam ademi, &
Parentem Consorte suâ orbavi. IN tam adverso
fato, hoc solum mihi potest jucundum esse, quod
Divi Parentes me Lodovicus, & Beatrix Medio-
-laneni. Duces genuere 1497. 3. Nonas Januarij

Family of Sforza

It was over the Gate of a Cloyster and a Monument of Curious workmanship, this Lewis was called the Moor from the Swarthyness of his Complexion and his Lady Beatrice was Daughter of Hercules Duke of Ferrara, by whom he had a Son named Francis w. Succeeded him with a second [Still born] Son in whose Birth the Mother died, of w. the Duke her husband was infinitely fond, and probably out of Tenderness to her Author of y. remarkable Epitaph. He dyed a prisoner of Warr in France, after w. in y. Infancy of his Son, the French Over ran & Seized the Milanese, it being driven out by the Emperor he Seized It. This Antient Family of Sforza ended in Francis last of y. Viscontis

M. Johnson Secr. also read 2 Riddles in Verse on a Candle, & an Ivory Combe,

2 Riddles Mss Poetry

Also an Impression of a Seale The Head of Marse in an Helmett, penes Crawford at 5955.8 Intaglia

M. Pincke Druggist was put up again in noiation, being proposed last Society.

Anthonij Thysij IC. Batavi Epitaphium Viri Incomparabilis
GERARDI. JOHANNIS. VOSSIJ. IZAACI. PATRIS.
Hoc tumulo plorat Pietas, & candida Virtus,
Et Luctu Pallas saxea diriguit:
Invida Mors ridet, ridet quoq, Vossius illam
Dum Calamo Mortem vincit & Ingenio.

Epitaph. in Ger: Johan VOSSIUM

The Rever. y. President in y. Chair, & Nine other Regular Memb. 20 Sept.

About 1104 Pp Innocent the 3. instituted an Order of Knighthood for converting Livonia, Liefland [whereof Courland is a most fruitfull Province situate with Semigallia, between the Baltick & Russia] called Ordo Ensiferorum Equitum, these were afterwards united with the Equites ordinis Theutonici, seu Livonici, and Gothardus Ketler Great Master of that Order was by the Authority & in the name of Sigismond Augustus Kg of Poland by Radzeuil Palatin of Vilna created and invested Duke of Courland & Semigallia for his Services done the Republick in their Warrs with the Russians in the Castle of Riga 1562. & Rex Vasallum jure beneficiario sibi Regnoq Poloniæ devinxit. and I think were confirmed with what border'd on Lithuania, to the Republick & Realms of Poland by the Treaty of Oliva 1660. and always esteem'd as a Fief to them belonging. altho the Swede overran It in 1658. In 1606 the D of Courland was of the Royal Family of Denmark, & had no Seat or Vote in the Polish Dyets. The Duke is of the House of Ketler stays Moden & and do homage to the Crown of Poland. his Residence is at Mittaw the chief of the Province of Semigallia.

Courland
Equit Teuton.

pat. 316. Just at Beaupre Hall in North:
M. Johnson Secr. com. part of a Lr. to him from B. Bell Esq. a Member describeing his Method of Registring in his Collection with his Reasons for useing such a Method : And also his Judgem. of y. Workmanship of the British Coines

L. from B Bell Rom. Coines of the British. M. Pincke abo.

M. Edward Pincke Druggist was upon Ballot elected & admitted an Honourary Member of y. Soc.

L. from M. Falkn. Poetry at

M. Johnson Secr. com. to the Soc. a latin Poem by way of Dialogue between the Rt. Bon. the Lord Tracey, & M. Newdigate of University Coll. Oxford entitled Calendarium Oxoniense 1733. on the Oxford Almanach being Lincoln Coll. and representing the Founder & some Presidents made by R. Grey D. Fellow of that Coll. sent him by M. Rt. Falkner a Student of the same Coll.

the Oxford Acc. on y. Almanach

NAUTILUS The following fine Lines in a late Poem entitled An Essay on MAN. in Epist: III p 13. Lin: 172

— Go! from the Creatures thy Instructions take;

Learn from the Birds what Food the Thickets yeild;

Learn from the Beasts the Physick of the Field:

Thy Arts of Building from the Bee recieve;

Learn of the Mole to plow, the Worm to Weave;

Learn of the little Nautilus to Sail,

Spread ye thin Oar, & catch ye driving Gale. when he cites Oppians Halieuticon L.1.

these Indian Characters are engraven on the outside on that part designed as the Lip of the Cup.

And a beautyfull Specimen of the Shell of that Fish in Mr Johnson the Secr Collection with these Indian Characters engraven on It when used by Thomas a Cup, wch he now shewd the Soc Occasiond his desireing some farther Act thereof, and at his Instance his Ingenious Frd Wm Bogdani Esqr (a Member of this and the Royal Soc) sent him in a Lr by the last Post in

Lr from Mr Bogdani dat. 15 Inst. Ansr to such his Enquiries. the above citation is thus introduced

MAN

See him from Nature rising slow to Art!

To Copy Instinct, then was Reason's part;

Thus then to Man ye Voice of Nature spake

Go from the Creatures thy Instructions take &c —

— Learn of the little Nautilus to Sail,

Spread ye thin Oar, & catch ye driving Gale. in his Lr Mr Bogdani gives an

the Figure marked represents the inside of the Shell when broken that marked the Entire Shell of the same Sort called the Thick shell'd Nautilus, used as a Drinking Cup, by ye Indians of Quality.

Account from various Antient & Modern Authors of the Nautilus with References to some Curious Drawings he has made of the Dicotomy or Section of a Shell of ye Fish, & the manner of Its Sailing taken from Specimens in the Museum of the Royal Soc. & that of the Learned & Honble Sr Hans Sloane Bart MD. President of the Coll of Physicians & of the Royal Soc. for the sd Secr. who having in his Lr acquainted him with this Soc Invitacon of that Learned and worthy Person and desired him to make It for him, he writes

Sr Hans Sloane a Member Last Wednesday I waited on Sr Hans, and acquainted him with the Nature & Order of ye Soc at Spalding & shewd him a List of such Members wch I could then recollect, most of which were of the Royal Soc. which pleasd him much, but expresd a Concern yt this Society should have been so long Strangers to him, and desird Me to acquaint the Society that whatever Knowledge or Information his rich Museum or himself can afford They may at all times freely command & that he should be well pleased of the Hon of becomeing a Member and being ranked with Body of Men of Learning and Ingenuity.

27 Septr 1733 The Revd. the President in the Chair and Nine other Regular Members.

Mr Bogdani's Drawings of the Nautili. & Descriptions by ye Greek Poets The Secr Mr Johnson shewd ye Soc. a fine Drawing of the thick shell'd Nautilus, from the Collection of Sr Hans Sloane Bart Member of this Soc. with an Elegant descript thereof by Oppian in Greek Verse, Halieutic. 1.1. ye 338. & Lippius latin Translation in Hexameters, Also a fine Drawing of the thin shell'd Nautilus, with his manner of Sailing Taken from Georgius Everhardus Rumphius D. Amboinsche Rariteit Kamer Amstel.m 1705 – with Callimachus's Greek Epigram, and Natalis Comes latin Translation, both in Hexametre & Pentametre Verse

Also a fine Drawing of the Section of thick shell'd Nautilus, from the rich & Invaluable Collection of the sd Sr Hans Sloane, with Plinys and Aldrovandus's Acct thereof from Aristotle &c all Drawn and written for the sd Secr by his Ingenious Frd Wm Bogdani Esq a Member of this & the Antiq & Royal Societies with wch that part of his Lr to the sd Secr was read illustrating the sd Drawings.

See for a farther description Dr Grews Catal: of the Museum Reg Soc. Lond fol 136. 137. & there Tab. 10 the picture of the Mailed Salor. Nautilus laminatus, not smooth but joynted like the Taile of a Lobster.

a Translation of Oppians Description of the Nautilus Ἔςι δέ τις γλαφυρῷ κεκαλυμμένⱺ ἱ 338
attempted by a Member of the Gent Soc.

Within a Curious, Concave Shell conceald
There lyes a certain Fish; whos Form reveald
The Polypus resembles, rightly He
's the Sailor calld by such as use y Sea:—

He dwells upon the Sands at bottom there,
Yet sometimes rises to the open Aire,
Swift seeks the Surface, but reverts his Shell,
Lest watery Weight his Energy repell:
But soon as Amphitrite he can gain
the Waive Superiour in thy noisy Main,
Instant he turns himself, & swimms no more
But seems as Sailing to some distant shore,
Stretches his Limbs, as Tackling some applys,
With some the Stream like busy Oares he plys,
Expands a Membrane thin, but strongly joynd,
Which gathers up, and swells out with the wind—

Thus thrô a thinner Medium he Enjoys
a ffresher Aire, and wholsom Exercise:
But hovering if oer head the Osprey fly,
Or other danger threaten, eer too nigh
The wary Nautilus with prudent speed
Draws in his Tackle, weightyer waves Imried
Streight fill his Shell, So save yᵉ subtle Fish
By Sinking him down to his deep Abyss—

Hence were Wee bold in hollow Barks to saile
Spread the thin Oare, & catch the driving Gale—

The manner of the Nautilus his Sailing as de- scribed by Dr Rumphins.

Y. Piso in his Edition of Bontius de Re Medica & utriusq Indix rebus Naturalibus in folio. penes Johñm Green MD. S GS Sor. Has a Drawing somewt like yᵉ but It stands wrong to ans the Design being Reversed his Cut is taken chiefly from Pliny whom he cites, but affirms he had seen yᵉ fish himself & felt thᵉ painfull Tingling effects of It upon his hand, so violent as almost to throw him into a Feavour.

These Nautili when petrified are what Wee call Nautilites, & Cornua Ammonis, by the Vulgar Serpens and Snake Stones. Y. Lyster de Cochlear. p. 205. Tab. 6
Illyds Litho Phylac Britan class. IV. p. 5. Tabb. 6. 7. and are supposed to have been real Snakes turnd into Stone By the miraculous power of a Saint

Mr Dotners the Secr Son a Member of this Sor. presented the Museum with a Cast from the Impression of a Curious Seal of that Son Sᵈ Sᵗ George Beaumont Baronⁱᵗⁱᵒᵗ he has the honᵗ of being related containing 42 different Coats of Arm & quarterings of Exquisite workmanship

also another made by him at the instance of the Sor. of a large full faced Antique Busto en Medaglion of Seneca the philosopher from Mr Bells shewn here 6ᵗʰ Instant.

The Operator brought in the Chameleon (wᶜʰ has been damaged, repaired & fitted up neatly in Spirits.

Mr Pincke a Member of this Society made his Donation of the State Poems in 4 Voll. 8vo —

The Revᵈ Mr Ray a Member presented the Museum with a Curious Lusus in an Ash bow—

Mr Cox a Regular Member notified to the Society that Thomas Wallis of Stamford MD. had accepted their kind Invitation to become a Member of this Society.

1733   Mr Johnson

Ægyptian Alabaster Statua duplex Maris & Fœminæ in a Lr from Mr Bogdani with Drawings

The Seer sheew'd the Socty a Drawing of an Idol and comunicated part of a Lr to him from Wm Bogdani Esqr a Member wch made the said drawings wherein he says: It was sent by a Gentleman at Venice to his Frd an Aporti in princes Street Stocks Markett London

The Venetian had it from Egypt by way of Turkey, it is of the exact Size of the Draught & carved in Alabaster but now grown of a reddish brown colour, the two drawings are the two sides of One Statua Back to Back & have but one pair of Leggs and Armes to both the Venetians esteem it to be a Dio Adamo or God Adam, saying that the Iews have a Tradition that Adam when first created was thus with Eve at his back but that God finding that not a proper Position for a Man & his Wife cut them asunder, whatever the Iews Opinion of Adam may be, I do not esteem this to be their Dio Adamo; others call it a Ianus but I think with as little Reason. The Caracters are very fair, & exact in the Draught, I having first rubbed them off upon paper & from thence traced them upon the drawings. I have shewed these Inscriptions to several Linguists who are at a Loss to read them, some say they are the antient Persian others the antient Chaldaick, but from the Great Affinity with the Arabick I esteem them to be that antient Character tho I am not versed in that Language any more than by Sight. Sr Hans Sloane esteems them to be an Ægyptian Abraxas. If I may be allowed a Conjecture this may phaps be an Idol adored by the Zabij mentioned by Spencer in his Book de Legibus Hebræorum Lib 2 whom he thinks with Scaliger to be a Sect of the Chaldæans Ægyptians, Nabatæi, Charanei, Syri &c & whose Superstition had infected most of the Eastern Nations, & quotes from Sharestone "Zabij cæli exercitum et sydera colebant tanquam numina, mentibusq divinis animata. & in another place he says "Chaldæorum veterum religio circa Solem Lunam, "Sydera Tellurum, forsan & eorum Symbola, versabatur. Now this Idol has on his Breast the representation of the Sun Moon & Stars which are doubtless placed there by Religious Superstition. The same Spencer Lib 2 Cap 4 de Lege Paschatis. — "Superest jam ut Leges "eas singulatim exequar, quas Deus, ad seculi superstitionem coercendum, & Zabiorum ceremonias "abolendas, dedit. and Sect 1. ejusdem Cap. "Hoc itaque remedio usus est Deus, ne superstitionis "ejusdem scabies Israelitas ureret, agnum illum masculum, quem Ægypt inter numina sua — "præcipua coluerunt, solenniter mactari, et ædium postes agni sanguine aspergi jussit. nam inde "facile cognoscerent Israelitæ arieti nihil inesse divinitatis & animal illud tam contumeliose "tractando se non minus ab Ægypti superstitione quam servitute recessuros indicarent. This Idol being thus clothed with the Lambs Skin confirms me something more in this conjecture, unless it may be objected as improper to represent about their Idol the flay'd Skin of a Beast held by the Devotees in such profound veneration. Whatever this Idol is the Inscription will probably discover I should be glad of your Opinion & the rest of my worthy friends of the Society & especially to have the Construction of the Inscriptions if possible. for those seem to be the most extraordinary

Characters ony Pedestal of ye Ægyptian Alabaster Statue or Idol.

on the Male syde of this Statue or Idol

On the Female syde

Description of this

On the Male Side is represented an old Man (standing on a Square pedestal whereon the Characters marked above are engraven) wth a long flat cut beard, a Chain round his Breast the Sun on his Stomach, 4 Starrs on his right Breast, a Crescent on his Left, thence to his Knees he's covered with a Sheep Skin

Herma=phraditical Idol.

On the Female Side a broad Faced open Mouth'd Woman, having a broad Ribband twisted over her haire changing spread upon her Shoulders, the same Chaine on her neck, the hind Leggs of the Sheep Skin tyd over a short Slit petticoat & that on a nother reaching to her knees with a deep fringed Howerd Border. the same Leggs and Armes serve both wch shews It intended for an Hermaphrodite, ye Woman has full Breasts.

36

Also a Dialogue in Hexametre Latin Verse between Wm Haslewin: 97. *Poetry*

Wm Bradbridge & Thomas Kilyard all Lincolnshire young Gent

of Mag. Coll. Oxf spoke in the Theatre at ye late Act. *Anthromania*

entituled *Anthromania. Sent by Mr Richard Falkner of Linc Coll:* L^r from
Mr Falkner

cleverly describeing the Beautys of Flowers, particularly of Auriculas and

Carnations & shewing the manner of Improving them, but Satyrizing too

great an Expence about them, called also Τυλιπομανια for the Excessive fond-

ness the Dutch have for that Flower, & ye Story told of It's roots boyld for Oynions, *Vegetables*

after the Horatian way in few words but very pleasantly and genteely.

The S^d Secr. brought a Large Root suppos'd to be Urticæ Urentis, Ligneous, & curiously fibred.

Saml Sharpe a Gardiner, brought 4 Apples of Equal Size growing in Forme of a Calthrop,

3 will be ye Base, and one at Topp, turne 'em as you will; & appear as in the Margin.

Mr Stagg the Soc^s Gardiner shew'd there many beautyfull Auriculas now in blow in Potts

The Rever^d: the President in the Chaire, & Eight other Regular Members . . . . *Octob. 11*

Mr Johnson Secr. com^d p^t of a L^{tr} from Mr Bogdani a Menu^s dat from ye Tower of Londⁿ 4 Octr instant, in L^r from M^r
Bogdani

wch that worthy & ingenious Correspond^t writes - They are now pulling down St Georges church

Southwark in order to rebuild It, wherein ye middle of the Wall of the Tower of that Steeple was

found ab^t a 14 dines an Inscrib'd Stone the Height of which was 11¾ Inch^s Breadth 9 Inch

Thickness 3 Inches the Lines of the Inscription ab^t 2 Inches distance from Each other, there

was a Stone placed before It as if to preserve it. It seems (says that learned Gent) to Me

as if but part of an Inscription, & that there were more Stones joyned together to make It up,

a Corner was broken in taking It down, 'tis there now in poss^{on} of the Clke of St Thomas's *Inscripcōn*

Hospital. The Inscription as hereunder —

The Revd Mr Ray V^P and Nine Other Regular Members — *18 Oct^o*

Mr Jackson a Member commun^d to the Soc. an Ingenious reply in Verse by way of L^r from *Epistok*

the Lady in France to Mrs Willes of Exton in Rutland Shire to her ludicrous answer

to wch the Ladys 1st L^r of Thanks for a wrought carpet were com^d 30 Augst last. with the Conceit

but most Elegant L^r in prose in wch Mrs Willes enclosed this reply to Mr Jackson L^r from Mr Falkner

wch were read and much entertain'd the Soc. as did a Poem at ye Oxford Act *Hortus
Botanicus
Danbeianus*

on ye Restoration of the Physick Garden there by the late Dr Sherard ye found^g

a Botanical Professorship, wrote in beautyfull Latin Alchaicks & Sent by

Mr Falkner of Lincoln Coll. to Mr Johnson a Member, & by him Communicated. *Danvers Earle of
Danby founder*

The R^t Honble Sr Henry Danvers Earle of Danby Baron of Dauntesey Ld President of *of ye physick
Garden*

Minister Govern^r of Guernsey one of his Maj^{ts} Privy Councel & Kn^t of the Garter founder *Oxford.*

of the physick Garden without ye East Pale of Oxford antiently a Cimeterie for the Jews in that *1632.*

City the Wall & Gate whereof cost him ab^t 5000^l GLORIÆ DEI opt. Max. Honori Caroli Regis

Dued Baron 2 Voll. 417. In Usum Acad. & Reipub. Henric Com^s Danby
D D MDCXXII.

Cast of ye Fall of Phaëton

Mr Johnson also shew'd the Soc. a Curious large Oval Cast of the Fall of Phaëton

Hac etiam Eridanum cernes in parte locatum
Cœli funestum magnis cum Viribus annem.

Seale of Upwell all Sts Church.

And the Impression of an Oval Oval Seale, wherein the Trinity is represented as Usualy by a Venable Antient Man with a Bird on his Breast & X'on the t between his Knees. placed under an arch of spiracled work. the Inscription

𝔰𝔦𝔤𝔦𝔩𝔩𝔲 : 𝔠𝔬𝔪𝔢 · 𝔢𝔠𝔠𝔩𝔢 · 𝔬𝔦𝔲 · 𝔰𝔠𝔬𝔦𝔭 𝔡𝔢𝔲𝔩

Sigillum Commune Ecclesia Omnium Sanctorum de Upwellis.

as Mr Saml Massey reads It, who says It's in his posson, and of Brass. and found at denham near Wells, in Norfolk, not far hom Wisbeach in Ely Isle.

Mr Johnson Secr read to ye Soc. hom a Lr to him dat 15 Inst from Beaupree Bell Jnr Esq a Member his Translation of the celebrated Epitaph at Farlam in the West Marches toward Scotland, near Naworth Castle very Faulty & Imperfectly published in Camden's Remains pag. 400. whereof this is the Correct & true reading

Epitaph of Johny Bell & Bs:lla Latin transt.

John Bell of Breken-brow ligs under this Stean: Ipse Caledonijs Bellus bene notus in Oris
Four of mine een Sons laid It on my Weam.   Mole sub hâc, Nati quam posuere, cubo.
I lived all my Dayes but sturt or Strife,   Mensa parata mihi, mihi semp amabilis Uxor
I was man of my Meat, & Master of my Wife.   Et placidæ Noctes, & sine Lite Dies.
If Thou'st done bett in thy time than I've done in mine,   Heus, bone Vir! Siquid fecisti rectius istis
Take ye Stean off o'my Weam & lay It upo' thine.   Hoc Marmor tibi do, quod tegat ossa,
                                                                        Libens

ABp Cardinl & J. Kempe & Tho. Kempe Ld Bp of London

The Revd Mr Ray com'd a Lr hom the Revd Mr Saml Pegge a Member wherein he says he has written the Life of Cardinal John Kemp & his Nephew Thos Kemp Bp of Lond" both in the reigne of Kg H.VI. desireing farther Inform abt ym ye Lr is dated hom Godmenham in Kent 15 Inst.

Amores Plantarum by Professor Hadrian Vn Royen.

Mr Jere Green shew'd ye Soc. Adriani van Royen Carmen Elegiarum de Amoribus & Connubijs Plantarum quum ordinariam Medicinæ & Botanices Professionem in Batavâ, quæ est Leyden, Academiâ, auspicaretur, dictum. 19 Iunij 1732. in 4o an Elegant Poem.

25 Octobr, The Revd Walter Johnson LLB VD & eight othr Regular & on:hon ye Member

Antient Extract of Antiquity Spalding 1531.

Mr Johnson Secr: shew'd the Soc. an Extract engrossed on parchmt of the Anticianity of the Court of Spalding cum Membris 14th year of the priorat of Nicholds Lord Prior of Spalding (as he conceiv't) A Dm 1476. and read & explain'd Several of the Articles to ye very remarkable & Shewing that great Care was then taken that the Laws should not be broken unpunish'd within this Manr this was in the 22 year of the Reigne of King Henry VIII. Anno Dm 1531. in part worn allmost out.

[Several lines of medieval Latin court-hand record entries follow, each ending with abbreviated sums]

Autient
Extract
of
Amerciam[er]

Spaldyng
1531.

Dñs Johñs Pittoll quia merserunt ſpinā maijs apud ffulnoy — vjd — · · · · · & alijs ſitr

Dñs Robto Orustow quia non mundit q̃ ruſtat ſuo ad guſtand doīno iijd · · · · · · & aliis ſitr

Dñs Thoma Rowy quia moluit coronā ad ſinū ſuū ꝑprivt · · · · iijd

Dñs Thoma Edundoſſon quia cuſtodiv guſtavs guttus cuiſoñ ex coīa õũoſ vjd & at ſitr

Dñs Thoma Roro quia cuſtodis vnū lo Ex Oẽynſtok nd tod bra adr ꝗno no iijd · · · · & at ſitr

Dñs eodem quia cuſtodis domos noroſſat voc Soẽyndotts nd tot virt iijd · · · & at ſitr

Dñs Thoma Smyth de Dobyt quia vou ſup ſolit Otorknyght conú voluntatou ſuam vjd

Dñs Robbt ho lou de Said quia cuſtodi gnoid Jutrols Jao capt ffe vocū viam ad noviand crouroy vjd

Dñs Willo Hayplou quia nõ cuſtodi fouā ſuas ſufficienū feoõs · · · iijd

Plit in Cur Baron

Dñs Eruo Orustow quia fodr gnoudit guttus in tot coia ad ꝗno noo iiijd

Dñs Johñ hoznoy quia non vou adr woogrunt Johñ tolghoſt ꝗñoi ꞇ Willm ffoſſo doſ iiijd & ꝑlus at ſitr x̃t ijſt

Dñs Robbano Bodyſtard ꝑ duobs ſ iiij ꝑſud Johñm byng vjd

Dñs eod Robbano Bodyſtard ꝑ liueiuo contor davnd cū Johñ king iiijd

Dñs Johñ Cothordr ꝑ duobs diu vñis Thomam proost do plibo bñoſ lxd & at ſitr

Dñs Johñ byrſt quia non ꝑe oſt queſot duam vñis Simonem Wghrodo plibo tñoſ iijd

Dñs Robbo Rambar quia non ꝑt oſt queſt duam vñis Thomam maryoum do plibo debr iijd

Leta cū viſu fraſphe anno xxiijo

Dñs Robbo Orustow quia oſt toroi fraboos ꝑauiſ ꞇ contrudꝑauoem ſouoʳ Aſſiam — vijd & 2 at ſitr

Dñs Agnetts Edmard vidua quia oſt ſoroi lard dño ꞇ vroꝑ ꞇ vro couā Aſſiam vijd & 4 at

Dñs Robto byo quia oſt ſoroi tipletos dño ꞇ vrardi dño oꝑcoſſio ſouā Aſſiam

Cnou ꝑ mouſuꝑ ſigillat — iijd & de x̃ at ꝑ conſili delicto

Dñs ꝑroro do ffrynſhodo quia non fac fouā ſufficious adr oꝛ xxd

Dñs Row boÿ Cotott dogloſtono ꝑ ſouo — xxd

Dñs Johñ tolghoſtoʳ quia puñt vagabund opiſbou in ꝑſona dñi ouadoꝛo ſino oꝛdmiuaoo vjd

Dñs Thoma proost quia in Willm Olandr inſult feoit iiijd

Dñs Willo Olandr quia in Thomam proost Aſſaū ſouā iiijd

Dñs Gregoꝛy hoſſou quia oſt toroi obuygatoꝛ viomoy dñ iiijd & 2 at ſitr

Dñs Johñ tolghoſtoʳ quia puñt Dunbam duam iauo duboñs Albem ponbou
do Spaldyng ſouo tuſno aguā in toia duoi voc Maylandobſtupad d iouo cuſſo ſuo vjd

Dñs Agnetts Edmard vidua quia oſt voui buūꝗ tū poʳoro ſuo in ſoꝑali campis iiijd & d at 4 ſitr

Dñs Robbo Tholo quia cuſtodi gnoud ſtoꝗuilond int tot virt iiijd

Dñs Robto Colvott quia non oꝛcrous ſui offio gubas dñio put myar ſui iiijd

Dñs Willo ꝑayrū quia non mundit q̃ gubas dñio adr guſband ſuo duem iiijd & 2 at ꝑconſili

Sm hũie cxlt ꞇ xliijd

the Spine of an Echinus Marinus or Sea Urchin

Petrified looking like

Petri=
faction
of
Fruit

He also shewed the Soc. a most Curious Petrifaction of some Fruit or Fruit Kernel given him by the Revd & Ingenious Mr John Tattam Vicar of Whaplode who had it of a Sea Officer that brought it from the Coast of the Red Sea and sayd he took it to be a part of the Sea Urchin: But that the Tradition of the place where it was found is that ye Prophet Elijah travailing there ashd relief of a man wo was carrying a load of Dates in a Sacke, and wo: answerd him he had Nothing in it but Stones, then replyd the Prophet — Stones be They — And they instantly & miraculously became Stones, of ye Forme & size in ye margin This seems a Fruit or Kernel of a Fruit sticking to the Foot Stalke, rather than a Sea Urchin or any part of that Fish, according to all yt I have, or have seen of them. w

Lapis
Judaieus

Laws of Motion explained

Mr Grundy a Member shewed the Soc. a Diagram to prove the Laws of Motion and the Solution and Demonstration thereof was read, explaining the Figure chiefly applyd to the Motion of Water, for the right & proper direction of Dreynes. in a long Folio Ms. of his own composeing in Mathematicks.

Grimesby a Burgh Incorporate

The Revd Mr Brainsby a Member presented the Museū wth an Impression of an Antient Brass Seale of the Corporation of Grimesby an Antient Burgh in this County in ye Wapentach of Brodley & parts of Lindsey formerly an eminent & wealthy Port, of wch Camden takes no more notice than to ridicule the Tradition of Grymesby Havelock his royal danish pupill. But Mr Owen of the Middle Temple in his Edition of Ogilby Actual Survey of the Roads of England &c p 208. Says Grimsby is a Large & antient Town Corporate governd by a Mayor & 11 Aldermen 12 Common Councell men 2 Bayliffes an High Steward Recorder 2 Coroners a Town Clerk & 3 Serjeants at Mace. The Freemen Inhabitants elect the Members for parliament. &

Religious Houses

That this Town had antiently 2 Monasteries. vid Suprà 5 July last. where there is some Account given from Lelands Collectanea of the Abby of Wellho juxta Grimesby, and of the Canons of that church of the Order of St Augustin – v: Maddox Firma Burgi fo. 129. c. d; & a Nunnery there called Monialium Prioratus, mencõned in the same former minuttes

Castle

& a Castle.

Tis at present saith Owen very fair and flourishing, driving a Considerable Trade, chiefly in Coales and Salt. the Markets are on Wednesdays & Saturdays. the ffaires 6 May & 24 Augst in the Margin he gives the Towns Arms, Arg: a cheveron betū 3 Boars heads couped Sable, probably this bearing might be taken from part of their antient great

Brodley Woods

Seale here delineated representing a Boar hunting. the Burgesses claiming Right Under a Charter of K of Ed. 1 to hunt in certain Neighbouring woods called Bradley or Brodley woods part of the ffôrest of Brodley formerly so called abt 2 miles distant from Grimesby, the present Lord or Owner whereof pays the Corporaĉon some acknowledgemt in lieu thereof or for desisting from the use of that Liberty of hunting in his Woods or Prouends to ys day as Mr Brainsby informed us. A dt of the Impression of the Great, & Little Seale another of this

Seales & Armes

Mayoraltie

✳ SIGILLVM HAIORITATIS DE GRIHESBY

This Corporation hath been known in ye Records by all these appellations Communa. Communitas, Homines, Burgenses de Grimesby &c 19 Ed. 1. &c [1291] pd 50 li for the annal farme of this Town Mag Rot 19 Ed. 1. itt Lincolnia. m. 1. a. & so the next yeare. which was a large Summe in those Days. They had a Mayor before ys Kings reigne for in his 1 yeare Philipp late Mayor of this Town made a Recognicõn in ye Court of Exheq. ibm fo. 138. Fin: Communia 1 Edw. 1. Rot. 7. a that is AD. 1274. & in 52 yeare of his ffather H iii. Reigne 1268. a writ issued to the Shireve of Lincolnsh. _ quod distring: Majorem & Sex de dicioribus & discreciõribus Hominibus de Grimesby for 5 yeares arreares of ye ffarme of that Town. Ex Memorandis 52 H3 Rot 8. a. ibm fol. 159. This fferme of Grymesby pd to the K g was Land called the Demeane and certain Mills there vid: Madox ffirma Burgi fol. 251. 252.

The Rev.ᵈ Mr Walter Johnson LLD. V.P.d 14 other Regular Members and the Venerable Father Dositheus Archimandrite of the Convent of Pantocrator on Mount Athos & Brother Paissius his Chaplain & Mr Nicholas Drake his Interpreter. To whom by order of ý Soc. their Treasurer gave a Guinea as a present

99

Mr Johnson one of the Secr. of this Soc. Notified to them the Acceptance of the Honᵇˡᵉ Lewis Dymoke Champion of England as Lord of Scrivelsby in this County which was by the Soc. ordered to be made his Honour 6 Jan 1725/6 & he was declared a Member of this Society

He also shew'd the Soc. a drawing of the Monumental Statue of a Knight which formerly lay in Swineshead Abbey Church now placed in ý wall of an House built out of the Materials of that Abbey by a Lofton as seems by the Arms carved thereon, ỳ a cheveron in a bordure — and New fronted by an Oram or Orme as seems by an Arms carved over the door à Cheveron betᵉˣ 3 Escallops, This is now called Swineshead abbey Farme & the Estate of Wᵐ Cotton Esquire. there being No Coat of Arms on the Knights Shield It cañ be positively said whose Image It is but ỳhaps of Robert Gresley the Founder Or Albert his Son. Let. Coll. 2 V. 92. It was of the Cistercian Order & at ỳ Dissol. valued at 167. 15. 3½ Aug d. 1014 2. & founded as he says from the Peterb. Annals 1134. The Common Tradition is that King John was here poysoned by a Monk in the Sacrament, that learned & Industrious Enquirer John Leland in his Coll. 2 Vol. 3 Tom p. 416. says from the Annals of Osney Sub A.o 1216 Rex Johannes in monasterio de Swineshead, quod est in Provincia Holandiæ, intoxicatus est, ut dicebatur. Tho. Wykes is sayd to be the Author of those Annals who wrote abt 1290. but that Author, adds, continuo cœpit ex vio= lentiâ veneni contabescere, indeq, progrediens usq, Newark, ibidem post dies paucos expiravit. Hist Ang Ser. v. ỳ Wille Gale fo. 38. For the Martyrologist gives the Story at large, but a good deal Incredible, & that Prince was so Intemperate & loos a liver yᵗ It might be a Violent Surfeit, of wᶜʰ these Sickened, and to that (which Matt: Paris a Most faithfull & Judicious Historian of that time says was of Peaches) and his Concern for the Loss of his Military Chest in the Washes, wᶜʰ he there heard of; He being then but in an ill State of Health, His death seems rather to be imputable: besides he was Unboweled & Embalmed at Newark by his own Physicians, & had he been poysoned, Wee may Suppose H. III. his Son & Successor would have done Justice on the Murtherer, or made Some legal Enquiry as less after such a Villain Q: whether ý King could be poysoned before ỳ had stamped into ý Chalice (as pretended) & if before not his Chaplain

He also comᵈ part of a Lᵗʳ to him from Mr Rᵈ Falkner of Lincoln Coll Oxᵈ dated Hilary 22 ult wherein he writes. that his Tutor had shewn the Inscriptions under the Egyptian Image (comᵈ supra 4 Oct. ult) to the Arabick professor there, who says Some of those Characters are something like Arabick, but he believes them to have no Signification, but that they are Some conceit of a Semichristian Mr Nic.k Greenall says the characters looked like Arabick but could explain them

The Revᵈ learned Mr Mark Hildersley MA Vicar of Hitchin in Hertfordsʰⁱʳᵉ was at his own Instance proposed by Mr Johnson a Regular Member to be admitted an honorary Member of ý Soc.

Mr Johnson Secr. shew'd the Soc. a ỳfect plant root leaves stalk & seed Vessel composed of 3 thick 3 angular leaves or divisions wᵗʰ round seed of the Colour of Minium ground of the IRIS wᶜʰ root he presented wᵗʰ Some of the seed to ý Soc. & they were planted & Sown in ý Society garden

The Archimandrite Dositheus shew'd the Soc. his Credentials under the hands of their Graces the Lord ArchBps of Canterbury and Yorke and the Lord Bp of Duresme & many other learned Men. Also a Crucifix curiously carved in hollow wood out of Box with many parts of the History of the Life & passion of our blessed Saviour, & also 2 very neat peices of carving in the same wood fixed as in Two leaves of a 24 book with Iceing Glass before them the One Representing the Holy Virgin & Child with 12 small figures of Patriarchs & Saints, the Other Jesus Christ with a Book a ỳ Judgemt open in his Lap & 12 like figures, & hell or Monster's head underneath, a foliage runs round all ý figures as a Stem

Swines=
head
Abbey

Sᵗ Rob. Greisley
Founder's
Image

Kᵍ John
Sickend
there.

ỳ tale of
his being
Poysond,
examined.

de fructu Persicorū & novi cicecis Po= tatione nimis re= pletus febrilem in= de calorem acquiit fortiter & ardentᵉ
M Par. 384. 14—

Lᵗʳ from
Mr Falkner

abᵗ Inscrip.
under Idol.

Revᵈ Mr
Hildersley
proposed

Iris
Seed V.ỿl

Greek
Abbot

Curious
Carving

41

8 Nov.
1733.
The Reverd. the President in the Chair & Nine other Regular
Members present

The Reverd. & learned Mr. Mark Hildersley M.A. Vicar of Hitchin was put up again being propos'd last Soc.

It was proposed by the Reverd. the Presidt. of ye Soc. That the Venerable Father Dositheus Archimandrite or Abbt. of the Convt. of Pantocrator & Archdeacon or Superintendt. of all the numerous Convents there — And the reverd. aged Bro. Paissius his Chaplain a priest & Monck of the same Convent — And Mr. Nicholas Drake Merchte ~~a Native of the Isle of Zant their Interpreter~~ be admitted honorary Members

The Address of a Greek Abbt. & priest to the Society

of this Soc. at wch. they were last Thursday permitted to be present at their own Instance in the following words under their respective hands — (vizt.)

1733 Νοεμβ: 8 Β υλοχορίο Λεγομενό οπαλινυ, ς τες τιμιεῖ
Αρχοντες απο το λεγμενό χορίο

ὶ Λεγόμεναὶ Πατερες Λιγένονσας ς τες αρχόντες ετ ετες τος εργαρισιοσνς πολλά και ἐς λογό και μαι Εργό και τοι εναμεανι μεγαλι αντρμιβα και εκινὸς οπε ἐμπολγοανε ιδι αρπαι αρχοντες, αι οποι απεδιμεναι εβχλχοι χαρδιά ναιλι Χ'ταὶ Πατερει Αχαι να ιαδερλ'ται βαλεται Τα ονομασαθάς και ναμαιται λελεται τοι εγχαρισιόσται απο χαρδίας —

Λοῖθε Αρχιμανδρίλης απο τό ἄγιον ὄρος

Παῖσοσε ιλο μ'ναχο απο το αγιον ὄρος

Κχρολαὶ Δραχός απο τ Ζακινλο

εχυνός ὀ τό εὑράψί τό επανο

Dositheus Archim. of Pautocr. Paissius Priest & Mr. Drake.

And the said Reverd. Father Dositheus, Bro Paissius ~~& Mr Drake~~ Seign.r Dracotti were upon Ballott each elected and admitted honorary Members of ye Soc. accordingly

Column in memory of K.g Ed.1.

Dr. Green Secr. gave the Soc. a drawing of a Square Tuscan Columne abt. 15 feet high, on a plain near an Arme of the Sea call'd Solway Frith belonging to a Village in Scotland (Burgh on the Sands) erected at ye Expence of Hen Howard Duke of Norfolk, in the Year of our Lord 1685. with ye Inscription thereon sent him by Mr chr Fairchild.

MEMORIÆ ÆTERNÆ
EDVARDI I. REGIS ANGLIÆ
LONGE CLARISSIMI, QUI
IN BELLI APPARATU CONTRA
SCOTOS OCCUPATUS, HIC
IN CASTRIS
OBIIT
7. IULII. A.D. 1307.

15 Nov:
1733

The Revd. the President in the Chair & 7 other Regular Members.

Revd. Mr. Hildersly admitted

The Revd. & Learned Mr. Mark Hildersley M.A. Vicar of Hitching in Hertfordshire was upon Ballot admitted an Honorary Member of this Society.

Poetry

A Dialogue in Latin Verse Sent by Mr Rd. Falkner from Oxford entituled Pyrrho redivivus. part of those Spoken at the late Act there.

The Rev.d the Presid.t and Six other Regular Members   22 Nov.r
& one Honourary Mr   Iones Maister of Musick

Mr Iohnson gave the Soc. some Acc.t of the Prince of Orange from the Report of   **Prince of Orange**
a Man of Learning and Iudgem.t who waited upon his Highness in Holland
upon a Signal Occasion, wherein he shew'd his good Understanding
in a Lr from the Secr his Father from Lond.n

Also some Acc.t of the Proceedings at the Royal & Antiquarian Societies London

In this Month of Nov. as Mr Grundy a Member told us Mr Beetniffe of Warwickshire had Rooks or   **Rooks in Nov.r**
Crows hatched.

     29 Nov:

The Rev.d Mr Walter Johnson V.P. and Eight other Regular Members
The Treasurer com.d from the Secr his Bro.a a Poem by a Lady on the Choice she   **Poetry**
would make of a *Lover* – also some farther acc.t of the Proceedings at y.e s.d Soc.
sent him in a Lr from the said Secr at London

The Rev.d the President and Seven other Regular Members and Mr Marshall   **6 Dec.r**
Crawford Jun.r permitted to be present and also Dr Delamore.   **1733.**

The President shew'd the Soc. the Root of a Red Beet which was Raised from Seed in   **Red Beet.**
Mays Ground by him being of the deepest Crimson Colour, above 2 feet in length and
full Sixteen Inches in Circumference near the Topp.

The Secr. gave the Soc. some Acc.t of the Proceedings of the Royal Soc. & Soc. of Antiquaries.

Mr Rowland V.P. and Eight other Regular Members present . . .   **13 Dec.r**

In Sr Wm Dugdales 3 vol: of the Monasticon Anglicanum fo 368. is a picture etch'd by Hollar after another lost
of designe and a dialogue of the daunce of Machabree by dan John Lydgate Monke of St Edmunds Bury   **Mr West's don.**

Mr Iohnson Secr brought in 30 prints of Copper Plates in 2o paper but small size   **Machabree**
Etched by Wenceslaus Hollar a Noble Bohemian from the Machabre or
Daunce of Death painted by Hans Holbein and presented to the Soc.
by James West Esq a Member of y.e Soc. &of the Temple, Royal, & Antiq.n Soc.

Also Lambards Perambulation of Kent the Second Ed.n his present   **Lambard of Kent.**
of the same c. Mr West to the Soc. Publick Library

Also Dr Nutty of the Urinary Passages, Dr Short of Teas, Tunbridgiale. Her Tracts given by   **Physick**
several Members in 2o bound up together with J. Antonides vander Goes Ystroom.   **Ystroom.**

The s.d Secretary also shew'd the Soc. a Copy of King Johns Magna Charta engrav'd by   **Magna**
from one of the Originals in the Cotton Library, and printed off on Velom, w.ch they desird   **Charta R.l**
to have one Copy of the like for the Soc.

And several Specimens of antient MSS in the Royal & Cottonian Library proof   **MSS.**
plates of those to be inserted in the History of the former by David Casley Deputy Librarian of Both of those Libraries and a Member of this Soc.

And also an History and Genealogy of the Princes of Orange Nassau w. their Pictures   **Orange.**

     Coine of Allectus

a Copper coine as bigg as a Sixpence given the Secr. IMP C ALLECTVS P F AVG   Caput ad humeros Allecti radiatum.
& Figura Mulieris in utraq. manu aliquid tenens LAETITIA AVG int. S & B. Senatus Benignitate.
probably he might have then prevailed on the British Senate A.D 297 Imperij Sui 2.o to confirm his usurpation
as Oliver Cromwell and some other usurping Murderers have since had the same sort of Sanction to their sway

20 Decʳ
1733.

The Reverᵈ the President in the Chair and Eleven Other Regular
Members Present.

Diana
Venatrix

An Impression from an Intaglia of Wᵐ Bogdani Esq, representing the head
of Diana as an Huntress with an Arrow placed before her. She is
generaly represented thus with an Austere countenance. Hildebrand
in his Compend. 125. says she is called Ἀπὸ τȣ Διος, because Jovis filia

Vel quasi Deviana, quod per Devia vagaretur venatrix Dea. vel quasi Dea Jana, quæ
Luna est. he exhibits from Augustini a Gemm representing her naked with her
Hair tyd up in this Manner, and the same Sort of stern Visage, with a little Roe:
Buck in her right, and Bow in her left hand: Montium Custos, Nemorumq, Virgo.

Mr Weyman a Member of this Soc. shewd yᵐ the following Medals well preserv'd

1st a large Silver
Medaglion
on yᵉ taking
Hulst

a City besieged over It 2 Cupids holding yᵉ Belgick Lyon in a shield. NUNC·SEPES·HORRIDA·RUSCO.
under the same Arms surmounted of a Crown arches this Inscription surrounded by Vines fruited
D.O.M·ER·S. An·Chr. MDCXLV. Fr·H·Aur·Pr. P·F·I postquam victrices Bat. legiones, ausu post recuperatam
libertatem inaudito Fossam una Fluvios iv. β ipsa Fland. viscera traiecisset; Hulstam intra mensis spatiū.
æstate iam adultâ cinxit, oppugnavit, ad deditionē compulit. I.Looff. f.
Buno on Cluver p.s. calls Hulssa Cornelij Jansenij patria a Fœderatis Belgis anno 1654 subacta. I suppose a mistake for 1645.

2ᵈ a large Silver
Medaglion on
yᵉ marryage of
Wᵐ Prince of Orange
& Mary Dʳ of K C·1.
1641.

On the Marryage with the entire Images of Wᵐ Prince of Nassau & Mary Dʳ of K C·1. with Cupids
holding wreaths over them, and the holy Ghost descending as a Dove. on Her side in these Letters
Albionum genuit Rex me Summusque Monarcha, Carolus et Sponsam me Jubet esse Tuam,
                                                                    on this Side
Princeps me Henricus genuit fortissimus Heros, Nassovia, et Sponsum me Jubet esse tuum,
in exergue under a fine Landskip of the City of Londᵉ & country & their Images
Londini desponsati Wilhelm, et maria Aᵒⁿ 1641 12 mai.

Peace presenting an Olive Branch to Pallas who treads on the Neck of Bellona
behind her an Angell with a Sword, a Cannon & other Warlike Weapons, the Ægys lying by
& behind Peace, Ceres with a Cornu Copia full of Fruits, between them a boy holding a
bundle of Arrows. Over all Bellonam Princeps Pallas Pedibus terit, et pax
                      Floret et Alma Ceres confert savro Alite Fruges &
In exergue. Novi Imperii Auspicio Bono. — I Blum. Fe.

3ᵈ a large Silver
Medaglion of
K C·2. on
his Embarkg
for England at
yᵉ Restauration
1660

the Kings Busto in Armour with a spike, & Cravat, & yᵉ Order in Arms full face.
CAROLUS·II·D·G·MAGNÆ·BRIT·FRA·ET·HIB·REX.
the English Fleet as sailing on the Sea, Over It Fame with a Trumpet in her
right hand, and a Scrole in her left, flying in the Air SOLI DEO GLORIA —— round It
IN·HOMINE·MEO·EXALTABITUR·CORNU·EIUS. PSAL·89·& in Orange as
within a CONCH. S.M. is uit Hollant van Scheveling afgevaren naer syn
                    Conincrijken Aᵒ 1660. Iuni. 2.
It was formerly in 2 plates now soded together & hung by a King atop. Cast work.
of a very bold and high Relief on the Head side.

4th a large Silver
Medaglion of
K C·2.

The Kings Busto in the Toga, the Head wreathed wᵗ Laurel, same legend,
his Majesty standing by a Rock, ships Engaging, in Exurgue. PRO·TALIBVS·AVSIS
on the Naval warr wᵗ the Dutch, on: d wᵗ ships is seen as sinking.

5ᵈ a Circular Golden, representing the last Judgement, the fall, Death, Sin, the Sinner, Moses, & hell in Bas:
or gilded Medal INFELIX·EGO·HOMO·QˢLIBERABIT·ME·DE·CORPORE·MORTIS·HVIVS·RO·7 ⁑
                    NVC·INSITI·CHRO·Q·OLI·ERAT& LONGE FCTI·ESTIS·PPE·IN·SANGVIE·X·
the brazen Serpent. the Holy Lamb. EPIEZ (ᵗ)
a Man cloathed in hair, & the Dove proceeding as in a stream from yᵉ Lamb to yᵉ Mouth
of a Naked Man. a Skeleton under the feet of yᵉ Lamb — & strange Bird under that.
This is a Cast peice, the device very extraordinary, the design and execution of the
Workmanship not of the best taste.

44

In Silver, Profile Busto of K:C:1. Crowned, w.th the Coller of y.e Order, large laced Bened and Ermine Robes ※ I Could hear both Houses of Parl.t for true Religion and Subjects fredom &c ※ as enclos.d in a frame of Leaves & Roses – ※ a Representation of both Houses upper & lower as Sitting in Parliam.t the workmanship Especialy on the head side very good, It seems to be a cast.

6.th
an Oval
Medal of
K:C:1

The Usurpers head in Profile with a Wreath of Laurell tied w.th Ribbands. OLIVAR·D·G·R·P·ANG·SCO·HIB &c PRO. fine Drawing and workmanship. 4 in a shild Surmounted of the Emperial Crown of Great Britain in 4 Q.rs 1 & 4. the Cross of S.t George for England ✛ and of forreigne plantations ✛ 2.d Saint Andrews ✕ or Saltoyre for Scotland. 3 Irelands Harp over all in the Centre, The Arms of Cromwell, a Lyon Ramp.t in an Escucheon of pretence: Over y.e Crown. 1658, around. PAX·QVÆRITVR·BELLO.

on the Rim HAS NISI PERITVRVS MIHI ADIMAT NEMO.

Very well preserved and most excellent workmanship of old Simmons

7.li
a Gold
Medal of
Oliver
Cromwell
by old Simon.

Of the Size of a Crown 2 Scutcheons hanging as on a Wreath with Festoons of fruits & flowers 1.st Quarterly Scotland – 2 in one Q.r Franc. England y.e terly 3.d Ireland. in the other Scutcheon the Belgick Lyon with a Sword in his Dexter & Sheaf of Arrows in his Sinister paw under a Branch of Olive & Palme Crossing Each other – on an Escroul. BRITAN: BATAV: PAX
1667. CA

8.th
a Silver
medal on
the peace w.th
y.e Dutch
1667.

R.s. a Dutch and English Ship, crowned each with a Wreath of Laurell, as rideing amicably together, their Colours all out, y.e Rigging w.ll expressed, a very great peice of worke in a case turnd out of Box and lined with crimson Velvett. Tis remarkable that as the Palme & Olive branch cross each Other under the Arms above described, That the Dutch, who caused this Medal to be Struck, Attribute Victory to themselves & peace to the English or rather Scotch, for the Palme branch is made to bend under the Dutch Arms, and the Olive Branch under the other M.ts.

M.r Falkner:
Draw.g of a
coine of

Also a L.r from M.r Falkner as Ling Coll. Oxf.d with a Drawing of a Silver Consular coine of Cap.t Vejovis. &.4 a Quadriga. in Exerg: C. LICINIVS MAC.

C. Licinius
MACER.

The Presid.t brought a Windsor Bean plant branched out into Nine Stalks, & 6 Beanes in 70 Podds.

Windsor
Bean

Capt.n Pilliod V:P: and four other Regular Members present (Vizt.)
the Rev.d M.r Whiting, the Secr. M.r Johnson, y.e Treasurer, and Operator.

27. Dec.r

The Rev.d M.r Ray a Member communicated a L.r to him from the Rev.d M.r Pegge another Member of this Soc. dated from Godmersham 6 Inst. conteining an Abstract of the Life of his Grace the most Rev.d Father in God D.r John Kemp L.d A.B of Cant. wrote by him, & in some forwardness for the Press. a Benefactor to the University of Oxford. wherein that Author desires some farther assistance as to MSS. from the Members of y.e Society,

L.r from
Rev.d M.r
Pegge
Life of B.p
Kemp.

To this Abstract w.ch ends with that Arch B.ps translation to the See of London ab.t 1422 are Subjoyned many marginal & critical References for correcting the Errors in Other historians, but Kemp was afterwards translated to Yorke ab.t 1425 made a Cardinal ab.t 1439. and lastly B.p of Cant. ab.t 1452. he dyd 22 March 1453.

Law
Deed
of
Heoffm

Mr Johnson Secr shewd the Soc. a very small Deedpoll of Feoffmt of Simon Son of Hugh Gouch of holebech to Conan Letson Conano filio Lete & his heires of all that land lying by Holebech bank at Hassosh ditch collaterally between the std Bank and land of Maud the Daughter of the std Hugh Gouch. To have & hold of God, the B. Mary & St John & de frib3 de Schyrebech sbide deo Heredit3; freely quietly peaceably & hereditarily Yt paying yearely frib3 sdm Hospital de Schyrebech one penny at the feast of St Michl forall Services. in pure and perpetual almes, they to warranty agt all & sundrie pnsons Hijs testib3.

Skirbeck
Hospital

Robt Blund, Robt de Hotun, Tho: the Provost. Gilbert his Son. Peter Hamondsn. Adlard his Bro. Tho Wygotson. Simon his Bro. Tho. the Clerk & others. no date. tis well written on a Scrap of Parchmt & has had a Seal on a pendent Labell, yt Seal lost.

It proves there was an Hospital the Warden or Provost whereof was a Layman at Skirbeck in this County (the Donor was devoted) & to dedicated unto. no Reservoof Services to the Lord of wm the Lands wer Cautiously holden — & yt rent call SERVICIUM, as prestatiopecunia is sayd to be. Rent Service, yt Fealty implyd,

I take it to be of or abt the age of H. 3. Phapps abt the Yeare 1273.

Note Skirbeck is a Rectory and the parish Church dedicate to St Nicholas. Its parish Surrounds the Borough of Boston, whence that vulgar distich

Tho Boston be a proud Town
Skirbeck compasseth It round

Sr Wm Dugd. 2 Mon Angl. 547 says Sr Tho of Moulton dedit Religioni ie to ye Knights Templars Domum Hospitalis Sti Leonardi de Skirebeke in Pam Libro. Ac totum Manerium Suud de Skirbeke cum Suis ptinentijs abt 1230

Mr Taylor
the
Oculist

Mr Operator Cox comunicated a Lr to him from James Bolton Esq a Member dated frm Denver near Doronaut in Norfolk the 3d Inst. giving a long and particular Account of the Operations on Eyes performed by Mr Taylor the Oculist, particularly on a young Lady and on Sr Tho Hares Coachman at Downham before Dr Brown of Lynn. his prices from one Guinea to 100. according to the diffi-culty of the case and ability of the Patient. this paragraph in the Lr is remarkable — Dr Hepburn Dr Brown & all who Saw him Said
, They never Saw any thing like his performances. In the Evening
, He dissected two Eyes a Sheeps and a Calfs before ye whole Company
, wc were 15 — And with good Reason contradicted and proved the
, general recd Opinion concerning Sight to be wrong.

46

PLACE INDEX

Note that counties are named only for places which lie outside the three parts of Lindsey, Holland and Kesteven, as they existed in 1974.

INDEX OF PERSONS

Biographical notes are given where possible.

SUBJECT INDEX

acrostic, 30
alphabets, 1, 2, 15
amercements, estreats of, 38
ammonite, 8, 10
Anglo-Saxon script, 15
antiquities, Roman, *see* Boston, camp, Canterbury, causeway, Chesterton, coins, cup, Hainton, lamp, Lowther, March, medals, mosaic, shoe, Stukeley, urn, vessell, Wansford, Weldon
apothecaries, xvi; *see also* herbs, Roberts, small-pox
art; *see* bust, drawing, engraving, etching, wood-cut; coin, heraldry, intaglio, medal, seal; *see also* Aaron, block-print, copper-cut, *danse macabre, Imitatio Christi,* mortars, moth, sea-horse, sea-snake, Seneca, shell, Theodore, Tutbury, urn
artists; *see* Beighton, Bogdani, Callot, Catesby, Durer, Fletcher, Gossett, Holbein, Hollar, Kent, Kirkall, Le Blond, Marshall, Tysbrack, Stranovius, Teniers, Thornhill, Vertue
auricula, 12, 37
avocet, whilloc, xvi
bakers, marks of, xiv
bean, Windsor, 45
bee-orchis, xvi
beet, red, 43
beetle, xv
binding, medieval, x
——, sixteenth century, xi
botany; *see* auricula, bean, bee-orchis, beet, carnation, Carolina, conifers, drugs, flower-arrangement, herbs, hop, iris, larch, rhubarb, thorn-apple, tulip, tulipomania
box-wood, carvings, 41
bull, papal, 20
butcher-bird, greater, xvi
camp, Roman, at Wansford, xiv
carnations, 37
causeways, 'Roman', 5
caustic, use of in surgery, 24
chameleon, 31, 35
chantry, foundation-deed, 23
——, statutes of, 20
chapels, burial in, 3
coins, modes of recording, 33
——, experiments to test, 25
——, English, 11, 22, 32
——, Roman, xiii–xiv, 4–5, 16, 20, 32, 43, 45
conception, false, xvi
concert, xii, xiii, 1
conifers, Norwegian, 19
consanguinity, dispensation for, 20
coot, white, xv
copper-cuts by Durer, xv
cow, unusual weight of, 21
cup, Roman, 8
dancing, written record of, x
danse macabre, prints of, 43
date, petrification of, 39

Domesday, excerpts from, xi
draining, machine for, xi
duck-shooting, xii
eclipse, solar, xi, 13, 15
Egyptian statue, 36
engraving, by Vertue, xv
epitaphs, 5, 24, 33, 38
etchings, by Teniors, Callot, xv
Etrurian language, 13
eyes, dissection of, xi
——, operations on, 46
fens, diseases of, 12
——, drainage of, xv, 8
feoffment, deed-poll of, 46
flower-arrangement, 5
glass containers, 31
gout, cure for, 12
harpsichord, xii–xiii
heraldry, 4, 10, 13, 17, 20–22, 33, 35, 41
herbs, catalogue of, xii, xvi
'heroc', use of, 29
hop, hop-ground, xv
illumination, described, x
ink, red, recipe for, 29
inscription, 14, 35, 37, 41; *see also* Frampton, Saleby, Canterbury
intaglio, 16, 22, 29, 33, 38, 44
iris, seeds of, 41
lamp, Roman, xiv
languages, lost, 13
——, oriental, 25
larch-tree, xvi
lead ore, xv
lightning, effect of, 8
linseed oil, 24
locust, found in Lincolnshire, xvi
——, plague of, in Germany, xvi
manuscripts, abbreviations in, 26
——, illuminated, x, 8
——, specimens of, 43
——, lent by Beaupré Bell, 25
mark, notarial, 20
mathematician; *see* Clark, G., Grundy, J., Peper, —,
mathematics, problems in, 11
mechanics, laws of, 40
medals, 1, 4–5, 9–11, 18, 20, 23, 29, 31, 35, 44–5
members, new proposed, 28
meteorological instruments, x
microscope, 20
mortars, 8
mosaic pavements, xiv, 31
moth, drawing of, 14
needle-work carpet, poem on, 31
newt (evett), 20
oak, 31
oculist, operations by, 46
oratorio, poem on, 32
organ, jack, xi

Printed books referred to in introduction and text, a selective list

Ames, Joseph, *Typographical Antiquities, being an historical account of printing in England,* London, 1749, xv
block print, Mainz, 1459, xv
Caxtons owned by Maurice Johnson junior, xi
Chambers, Ephraim, *Cyclopaedia, or an universal dictionary of arts and sciences,* 2nd. ed., 2 vols. in fo. 1733–53, 25
Clark,? Thomas, ed. Newton's *Optics,* originally published 1704, issued in 1719, xii
Dugdale, William, *Monasticon Anglicanum, to which are now added exact catalogues of the Bishops of the several Dioceses to the year 1717,* fo., London, 1718, 43, 46
Gataker, Thomas, *Marcus Antoninus de rebus suis,* London, 1697, xii
Havercamp, Sigebert, *Josephus Flavius Opera Omnia Graece et Latine,* 2 vols. fo., Amsterdam, Leyden, Utrecht, 1726, 1, 29
Hearne, Thomas, *Duo Rerum Anglicarum Scriptores,* Oxford, 1732, xv
Hevelius, Johannes, *Selenographia sive lune descriptio,* Gdansk, 1647, xiv
Heywood, Thomas, *The Hierarchie of the Blessed Angells,* London, 1635, xii
Hickes, G., *Grammatico Anglo-Saxonico ex Hickesiano linguaram excerpta,* ed. E. Thwaites, Oxford, 1711, xv
Lambarde, W., *The Perambulacion of Kent containing the description, history and customs of that county, corrested and enlarged, to which is added the charters, laws and privileges of the Cinque Ports,* London, 1656, 43
London Cases of Controversial Divinity, 3 vols., 8vo, before 1732, 22
Luther, Martin, ed. *Psalms,* 1538, 9
Madox, T., *Formulare Anglicanum,* London, 1702, 32
Magna Carta, copy published 1732, 20, 43
Orlandi, Pellegrino Antonio, *Abcedario Pittorico Repertorium Sculptile,* Bologna, 1719; English translation, London, 1730, 26
Picard, Bernard, *Ceremonies et Coutumes Religieuses de tous les peuples du monde,* 4 vols in 7, Amsterdam, 1733–47, 21
Plautus, Titus, Maccius ... opera Dyonisii, Lambini emendatus, Paris, 1588, 13
Raphalengius, Franciscus, *Imagines* etc., Leyden, 1599, 11
Ray, John, *Synopsis Methodica Stirpium Britannicarum,* London, 1690, 12
Repertorium Sculptile Typicum, see Orlandi
Rutty, William, *Urinary Passages? (An account of some new experiments and observations on Joanna Stephens' medicine for the stone),* London, 1747, 43
Short, Thomas, *Tunbridgiale,* before 1732, 43
Stamford, Almanack, 1625, 2
State Poems, videlicet 1. Verses upon the sickness and recovery of Robert Walpole, 8vo. for J. Roberts, London, 1716, 35
Valerius Maximus, ed. J. Knobloch, Strasbourg, 1521, xi
Van Royen, Adrian, *Amores Plantarum,* Leyden, 1732, 38
Vander Goes, S. Antonides, *Ystroom,* 43
Weekly Miscellany, giving an account of the religion, morality, and learning of the present times, The, 2 vols., London, 1738 (R. Hooker), 6
Worde Wynkyn de, *Legenda Aurea,* London, 1493, xv